AGAINST THE RISING SUN

New Zealanders Remember the Pacific War

Also in this series:

'A Unique Sort of Battle': New Zealanders Remember Crete
Inside Stories: New Zealand Prisoners of War Remember
A Fair Sort of Battering: New Zealanders Remember the Italian Campaign
The Desert Road: New Zealanders Remember the North African Campaign
Hell or High Water: New Zealand Merchant Seafarers Remember the War

AGAINST THE RISING SUN

New Zealanders Remember the Pacific War

EDITED BY MEGAN HUTCHING
with Ian McGibbon and Alison Parr

FOREWORD BY THE RIGHT HONOURABLE HELEN CLARK

HarperCollins*Publishers*

in association with
the Ministry for Culture and Heritage

National Library of New Zealand Cataloguing-in-Publication Data

Against the rising sun : New Zealanders remember the Pacific
War / ‡c edited by Megan Hutching ; with Ian McGibbon and
Alison Parr ; foreword by the Right Hon. Helen Clark.
ISBN 1-86950-604-9
1. World War, 1939-1945—Campaigns—Pacific Area—Personal
narratives, New Zealand. 2. World War, 1939-1945—New
Zealand. I. Hutching, Megan. II. McGibbon, I. C. (Ian C.), 1947-
III. Parr, Alison. IV. New Zealand. Ministry for Culture and Heritage.
940.54260922—dc 22

First published 2006

HarperCollins*Publishers (New Zealand) Limited*
P.O. Box 1, Auckland

ISBN 1 86950 604 9

Set in Bembo

Cover design by Darren Holt, HarperCollins Design Studio
Book design by Dexter Fry
Typeset by Janine Brougham
Printed by Everbest Printing, China

Main front cover photo: Drying out on the beach at Malsi, Mono Island, after a wet night.
Archives New Zealand, WAII, 7/14, K1151/4, 10
Inset front cover photo: New Zealand troops on amphibious training in the Pacific. ATL, War History Collection, WH-0182
Back cover photo: RNZAF Corsairs off Guadalcanal, 1944. ATL, Evatt Collection, F-106417-1/2

In memory of my father,
Gunner I.H. (Ted) Hutching, 469552,
1914–1989
M.H.

Foreword

I am very pleased to welcome this book of personal accounts from New Zealanders who served in the Pacific during the Second World War.

Against the Rising Sun is the sixth in a series of books based on oral histories of veterans from the 1939–45 conflict. The seventh and final book will be about the experiences of men and women who served in uniform on the Home Front.

The Pacific War brought the fighting very close to home for New Zealanders. For the first time in our country's history, it seemed not improbable that we could be invaded by a hostile nation.

It was thus deemed essential that New Zealand took part in the war against Japan. The war in the Pacific brought us into sustained contact with defence personnel from the United States, an experience which was positive for most of those interviewed for this book. With the dropping of the atomic bombs on Hiroshima and Nagasaki, this war was to end in a way which heralded a new era in both warfare and international relations.

One of the joys of oral history is that it allows us to hear directly about the past. The rich memories recorded in this book give us insights into what it was like to take part in the amphibious landing on Mono Island while under fire from the Japanese, to attack enemy bases as part of the RNZAF, and to be on an aircraft carrier which was under attack from Japanese kamikaze aircraft. We can also read about the boredom of many aspects of military life, and how men diverted themselves with music, handicrafts and movies.

It has been said that the war in the Pacific is the 'forgotten' war, as the activities of those who took part have not been written about as exhaustively as have the ventures of those who fought in the European war. I hope that this book will go some way to redressing that imbalance.

I thank all the veterans who shared their stories with us. I congratulate Megan

Hutching and the very professional team in the Ministry for Culture and Heritage for producing this book. I urge New Zealanders to read *Against the Rising Sun* and learn more about the human dimension of this 'forgotten' part of the war. In doing so, we remember the sacrifices made by those who protected our small country so many years ago.

Helen Clark
Prime Minister

Contents

Preface   11

Glossary   15

Introduction: Battling the Rising Sun: New Zealanders in the Pacific War   21
   Ian McGibbon

Further Reading   51

'Everybody Became Prisoner of War'   53
   Ian Newlands

'Singapore on Fire'   71
   William Mitchell

'The Pacific Islands Were in Danger'   89
   Harry Bioletti

'The Mosquitoes Were Big'   105
   Doug Benge

'Hawaii's Been Attacked'   121
   Peter Renshaw

'Riding Beautiful Motorbikes'   137
   Rob McLean

'We Started to Flood'   151
   James Murphy

'Through the Shattered Palm Trees'   169
    Noel Rosoman

'Smoke and Flames from Burning Aircraft'   183
    John McKay

'Ralph Williams and His Tiger Rags'   199
    Ralph Williams

'We Strafed Down the Jungle'   215
    Richard Mapp

'Japanese in Large Numbers'   231
    Alan Roberts

'It was Mainly Air Raids'   245
    Thomas White

'We Loved Our Ship'   261
    Pita Tauwhare

Index   271

PREFACE

Preface

My father, Ian (Ted) Hutching, went away to the war in late 1942. He was an anti-aircraft gunner and was in New Caledonia for a few months before being invalided back to New Zealand, much to my mother's relief. She had three small girls and was pleased to have him back safe, if not particularly sound. Dad never spoke much about his time in New Caledonia, beyond marvelling at the size of the mosquitoes ('One landed on an airfield and was filled with gas before the groundcrew realised it was not an aircraft' was one of his few jokes about that time) and the fact that many American servicemen read only comics. For me, this book has been a journey of discovery about what the Pacific War was like, for as with many families, my siblings and I are part of one where 'Dad never talked about the war'.

Alison Parr recorded all the interviews for *Against the Rising Sun*. It has been a novel experience for me to edit interviews with people I have never met (with the exception of Harry Bioletti, who taught at Mahurangi College when I was a pupil there) and whom I know only by the sound of their voice on tape and by brief telephone conversations. It is a mark of Alison's talent and expertise that this has been such an easy process for me. To her go my heartfelt and very grateful thanks.

My colleague Ian McGibbon has done his usual excellent job of writing the introduction and giving me the benefit of his comprehensive knowledge of the Second World War. Neill Atkinson offered feedback on the accounts from naval servicemen. David Green has edited the text with skill and thoughtfulness, and Bronwyn Dalley, the Chief Historian, has offered her usual support and knowledge throughout the project. I am also grateful to Brenda Watson, who transcribed most of the interviews for me.

In order to find people to interview, I began by publicising the project and asking people who had taken part in the Pacific War to get in touch. I then sent them a lengthy questionnaire asking them about their experiences. I am extremely grateful to those who filled in my questionnaire either for themselves, or on behalf of someone else. I have also been fortunate to receive accounts from people of their experiences or their relative's experiences during the war, which I very much appreciated.

Previous page: *Men from the malarial control unit spray a pool in the Pacific. Note the shell-damaged palm trees.* ATL, War History Collection, F-41541-1/2

All the questionnaires and other accounts that I have received will eventually be deposited with the Alexander Turnbull Library in Wellington, where they will be available to researchers. The recordings of the interviews and accompanying material will be archived at the Oral History Centre at the Turnbull Library, where they will be available to researchers subject to any conditions placed on them by the interviewees. The words which appear in this book are just a small proportion of those recorded in the interviews. I have tried to preserve the informal language of the interviews because I wanted them to reflect how people spoke, but each has been heavily edited.

I must also thank: the Prime Minister, Helen Clark, for her continuing interest in this series of books, which she initiated; Katie Duke, for her terrific picture research at the Alexander Turnbull Library (ATL) and Archives New Zealand (ANZ); Heather Mathie and her colleagues at Turnbull Library Pictures; Vernon Wybrow and his colleagues at Archives New Zealand; Paul Restall at the Navy Museum; Matthew O'Sullivan at the Air Force Museum; Ray Ansdell for the loan of his father's photographs of Singapore; Linda Evans and the staff of the Alexander Turnbull Library's Oral History Centre; the team at HarperCollins for their support and expertise, especially Sue Page, who edited the text. And special thanks to Charlotte Yates, Jayne Wasmuth, and all my other friends who still listen with interest to my tales of war, and give me support and encouragement in return.

Megan Hutching
March 2006

Glossary

2NZEF	Second New Zealand Expeditionary Force
ack–ack	anti-aircraft (fire)
aft	at or towards the stern of a ship
Aldis lamp	electric lamp with shutters for sending signals at sea
ASC	Army Service Corps
barrage	barrier
Bofors	light anti-aircraft gun (Swedish)
bridge	elevated enclosed platform from which a ship's officers direct operations
Browning	a British machine gun
Buffalo Brewster	US monoplane fighter
bulkhead	vertical partition dividing a ship's hull into compartments
capital ship	a large warship such as an aircraft carrier or battleship
Catalina	US twin-engined flying boat
CB	construction battalion
chow	food
civvy	civilian
CO	commanding officer
conchies	conscientious objectors
Corsair	US single-engined fighter aircraft
corvette	small, fast escort ship
cruiser	high-speed, medium-sized warship with medium armament
daisycutter	bomb that detonates a few feet above the ground
Dakota	US twin-engined aircraft, mostly used for transporting personnel and cargo
destroyer	small, fast, highly manoeuvrable warship
Div	Division(al), in Pacific usually 3 New Zealand Division
drome	aerodrome

DSIR	(New Zealand) Department of Scientific and Industrial Research
dynamo	machine converting mechanical energy into electrical energy
foxhole	hole dug in ground for use as shelter or firing position
g	(acceleration of) gravity
glycol	liquid often used as antifreeze
Grumman Avenger	US carrier-borne torpedo and light bomber aircraft
Harvard	US single-engined training aircraft
howitzer	high-angle bombardment gun
Hudson	British twin-engined bomber aircraft
Hurricane	British single-engined fighter aircraft
Jap	Japanese
Kittyhawk	US single-engined fighter or fighter-bomber aircraft
LAC	leading aircraftman
LCI	landing craft infantry
LST	landing ship tanks
MC	Military Cross
Mitchell	US twin-engined bomber aircraft
mortar	short-range, high-angle bombardment gun
NCO	non-commissioned officer
OCTU	Officer Cadet Training Unit
Oerlikon	20-millimetre, quick-firing anti-aircraft cannon
P & T	Post and Telegraph Department
pinnace	small ship's boat
pipe	whistle used to summon crew on board ship
POW	prisoner of war
PT	patrol torpedo (boat)
PX	Post Exchange (military store)
RAF	Royal Air Force
RAP	Regimental Aid Post (first aid station)
RNZAF	Royal New Zealand Air Force

RNZN	Royal New Zealand Navy
revetment	a barricade against explosives, shells, etc.
Spam	tinned meat
(a)stern	after-end of the ship; opposite of bow
superstructure	the part of a ship's structure above the main deck
Tiger Moth	British biplane used for training pilots
Ventura	US light bomber and maritime reconnaissance aircraft
WAAC	(member of the) Women's Auxiliary Army Corps
WAAF	(member of the) Women's Auxiliary Air Force
Yale	US single-engined training aircraft
YMCA	Young Men's Christian Association
Zero	Japanese single-engined, carrier-based fighter aircraft

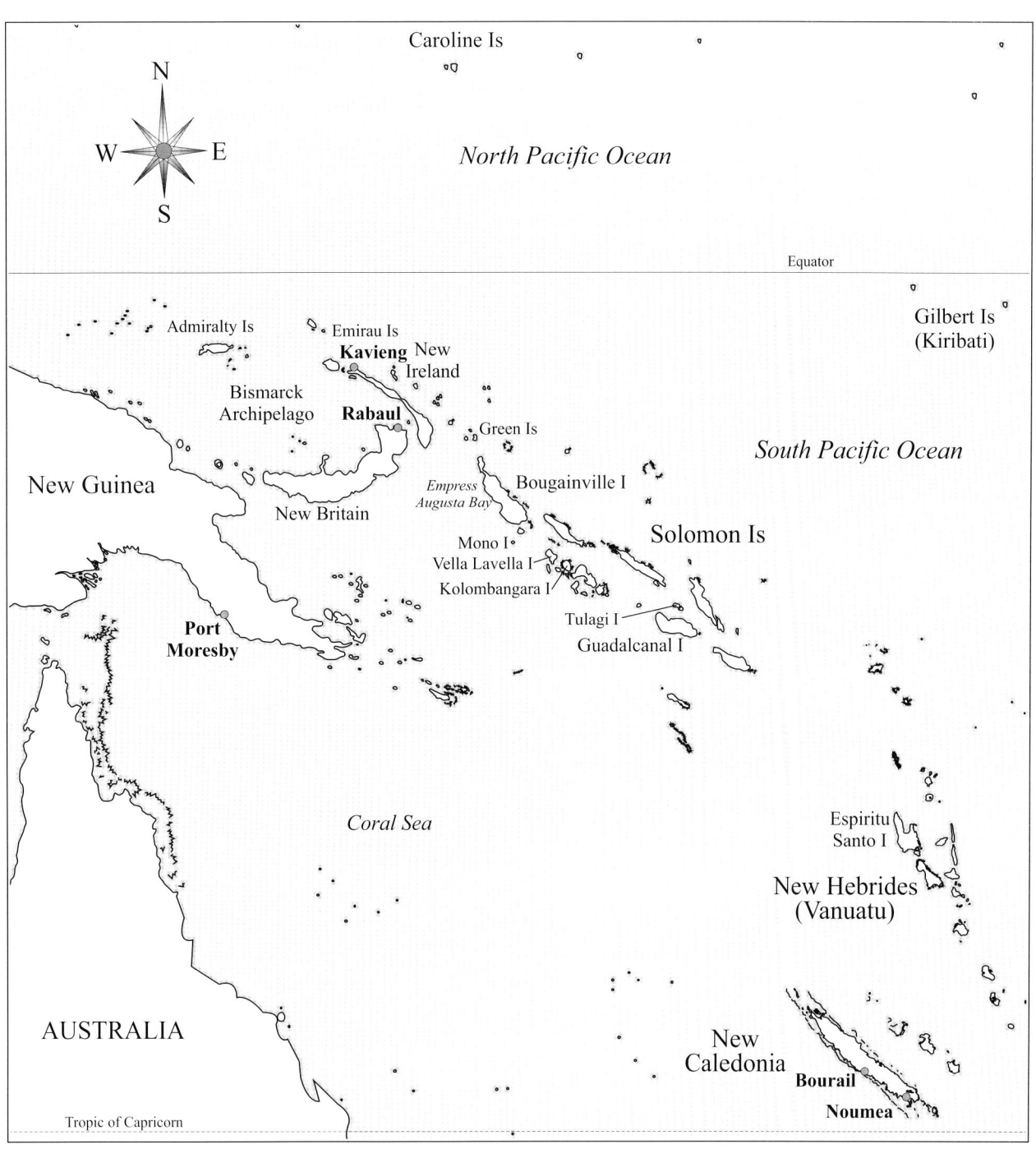

N
W   E
S

Caroline Is

North Pacific Ocean

Equator

Admiralty Is   Emirau Is   **Kavieng**   New Ireland

Rabaul

Bismarck Archipelago

Green Is

South Pacific Ocean

Gilbert Is (Kiribati)

Empress Augusta Bay   Bougainville I

New Guinea

New Britain

Mono I
Vella Lavella I
Kolombangara I

Solomon Is

Tulagi I
Guadalcanal I

Port Moresby

Coral Sea

Espiritu Santo I

New Hebrides (Vanuatu)

AUSTRALIA

New Caledonia

Bourail

Noumea

Tropic of Capricorn

INTRODUCTION

BATTLING THE RISING SUN: NEW ZEALANDERS IN THE PACIFIC WAR

IAN McGIBBON

FOR DOUG BENGE, the dangers of war became very real one day in early 1943. Standing with his head in the astrodome of a Hudson bomber, with the task of directing the pilot on evasive action, he had a grandstand view as six Japanese fighter planes swooped down. The sight of the red roundel identification sign of a Japanese Zero whizzing past was a vivid reminder that this was no training mission. The lives of the New Zealanders hung in the balance, for their lumbering Hudson was no match for its attackers. As the pilot thrust the plane into a dive, the Japanese followed it down. Bullets could be seen spattering the sea ahead as the enemy pilots tried unsuccessfully to hit the plane as it swerved in response to Doug's urgent calls. After levelling off near the sea, the pilot managed to climb back up into the enveloping security of a cloud. Scurrying from one cloud bank to another, the Hudson made its escape.

Doug was one of many thousands of New Zealanders who took part in the Pacific War, which began when Japan entered the Second World War in December 1941. The ocean that was named for peace became an arena of war. It was a conflict fought on a vast scale over huge distances, with great armadas of warships ranging the ocean and men fighting each other in desperate actions on small island outposts. It was also fought with little concession to humanity. On both sides the rules of war were commonly ignored. Racial hatred added an edge of bitterness that was not apparent in the fighting in which New

Previous page: *A soldier looks at dead bodies on a Pacific beach.* ATL, War History Collection, F-41854-1/2
Right: *New Zealand servicewomen in a laundry, New Caledonia.* Archives New Zealand, WAII, 7/9, 888

Zealanders participated in the Mediterranean and Western Europe. For a small island state in the South Pacific, it was a war that had profound consequences. It brought the danger, for the first time in New Zealand's existence, of invasion by a hostile power, and prompted an unprecedented mobilisation within the country. It changed the international politics of the region in a way that still endured more than half a century later. Finally, because of the use of atomic weapons it was a war that ended in a fashion that heralded a new era in warfare and raised profound moral issues.

Although several hundred women served overseas in the Pacific theatre—WAAF clerks with the air force, WAAC voluntary aides in Tonga, Fiji, and New Caledonia, and army nurses in New Caledonia and on the hospital ship *Maunganui*—the vast majority of New Zealanders who took part in operations against Japan outside New Zealand were men. In this book, 14 of them relate their experiences. They include some who suffered in the disasters that happened to Britain as Japan rampaged through Southeast Asia in the early months of the conflict. Bill Mitchell and Ian Newlands served as airmen in Singapore, and the latter had the misfortune to spend four years as a prisoner of war, mostly in Japan. Two-thirds of the men interviewed here took part in fighting much closer to home, in the Solomon Islands. Harry

Bioletti, Rob McLean, Peter Renshaw, Ralph Williams and Noel Rosoman were soldiers who served with the Second New Zealand Expeditionary Force in the Pacific. Doug Benge and Richard Mapp were part of the Royal New Zealand Air Force's substantial contribution to the fighting in this area. The navy is represented by James Murphy and Thomas White. An interesting perspective on the operations that led to the defeat of Japan is provided by Alan Roberts, one of the few New Zealanders to serve in the central Pacific. Thomas White, Pita Tauwhare and John McKay describe their experiences aboard warships in the huge Allied naval array that bore down on the Japanese homeland in 1945.

SETTING

THE PACIFIC WAR BATTLEFIELD stretched from the Hawaiian Islands in the east to the border between India and Burma in the west, and from the subarctic Aleutian Islands in the north to the Solomon Islands in the south. Within this huge arena New Zealanders fought Japanese in three areas mainly—in Singapore, in the Solomon Islands, and in the waters surrounding Japan. All three places had an exotic quality for New Zealanders in the early 1940s, for they lay in a part of the world that was unfamiliar to a population predominantly oriented towards Europe. Singapore was a backward city with a heavily polluted and foul-smelling river. The Solomons were even more backward. Both were trying for men unused to the persistent heat and humidity of the tropics. Relentless rain often made life difficult. Tropical storms that could appear with startling suddenness put all who flew in aircraft at risk.

For men with no venomous creatures in their homeland, the jungles of the Solomons were places of anxiety. Snakes were especially abhorred, while spiders, scorpions, centipedes and other insects made life uncomfortable. Leeches were another unfamiliar nuisance. Rob McLean and Peter Renshaw both have vivid memories of the land crabs. It was no joke to wake up with one of these 'horrible things' near you, especially because they nipped. The rustling of thousands of them on the move was a common sound at night. In most areas, mosquitoes tormented the men. 'We would go to the toilet and they used to tear into your backside,' Rob McLean recalls. 'They were everywhere.' There were so many in one place on New Caledonia that 'some of the boys went a bit troppo'. The mosquitoes were especially troubling because of the danger posed by malaria. Men took Atebrin tablets to suppress the effects of the disease, going yellow as a result; and they had to cover up after sundown. But malaria was only one of the threats to the health of the New Zealanders. Prickly heat, tinea and festering sores were constant problems, while hookworms were waiting for anyone foolish enough to walk barefoot on land. Dengue fever was endemic, and men also contracted hepatitis. Elephantiasis was another menace. Diarrhoea could also make life unpleasant, especially for airmen obliged to spend hours in cramped cockpits.

Superimposed on these dangers were those presented by the enemy. Invariably depicted by Allied propaganda as small, bucktoothed, bespectacled,

Sign at New Zealand Divisional Headquarters on Vella Lavella. These signs were posted around the island. ATL, War History Collection, F-20417-1/2

and scarcely human, the Japanese were regarded very differently from the Italians and Germans. Their behaviour aroused a great deal of apprehension among those who faced them, especially airmen who might fall into their hands after being shot down. There was evidence of the maltreatment, even murder, of prisoners, and of atrocities among the populations brought under Japan's control, especially the Chinese. The Japanese seemed to fight in an alien way that was exemplified by their suicidal determination, a product of a military code and societal values that emphasised the dishonour of surrendering. This was underscored late in the war when kamikaze pilots attacked Allied ships. Soldiers who served in the islands were conscious that Japanese could be close by in the surrounding jungle. They proved an elusive enemy when the New Zealanders were tasked with seizing or clearing islands, and some remained hidden even after the fighting ended. For most troops in Singapore and the Solomons, the Japanese made their presence felt in air raids. These were common in 1943 but ended in February 1944, when the Japanese pulled their surviving air units back to the central Pacific.

In contending with the problems the theatre posed, the New Zealanders found themselves in an unfamiliar environment. Initially, in Singapore (and later in Burma), they were attached to or served alongside their traditional allies, the British and Australians. But New Zealand soon had to adjust to the reality that the war in the Pacific would be dominated by the Americans. New Zealand was included

LAC Bill Mahood bandages a child's foot, Espiritu Santo. ATL, RNZAF Collection, F-106383-1/2

in the US South Pacific Area, part of Admiral Chester Nimitz's vast Pacific Command. Although New Zealand retained control of its land forces at home, those who garrisoned islands or fought elsewhere in the South Pacific came under the American vice-admiral commanding the South Pacific Area. For the first time New Zealanders fought without the comforting presence of the British. They had to adjust to American command and ways of doing things. At times New Zealand officers commanded Americans, and the troops who interacted with the 'Yanks' generally found them 'good blokes', although the ostracism of black soldiers by some was regarded with distaste by the more egalitarian New Zealanders.

In Singapore, the New Zealanders had little to do with the local inhabitants, who were mainly Chinese. There was more contact with indigenous inhabitants in the South Pacific, especially in Fiji and to a lesser extent in New Caledonia. There was also a French population in the latter, but the language barrier hindered interaction for all but those like Rob McLean who mastered some French. In the operational areas in the Solomons and New Britain the locals were less apparent, although they occasionally appeared. Bill Mitchell remembers them hawking souvenirs to the soldiers, while Richard Mapp noted that the women and children, in contrast to their menfolk, carefully avoided the camps. Many of these local inhabitants were in noticeably poor health.

PRELUDE

J APAN'S ENTRY TO THE WAR came as a shock, yet it was not entirely unexpected. Almost from the time that Japan defeated the Russians in 1905 the possibility of war with the Asian nation had been recognised by some in New Zealand. Japan's imperialist aims seemed likely to bring it into conflict with Western powers. For the time being the dangers were lessened by Japan's alliance with the British Empire, but in 1921 that arrangement came to an end. Worried by British weakness in the Pacific, New Zealand governments supported British plans to deal with possible Japanese hostility. They contributed more than £1 million towards the construction of a major base at Singapore. In the event of war with Japan, a British fleet would come east to the base from Europe and the Mediterranean to counter a Japanese move to the south.

Long before this Singapore strategy was capable of being implemented, aggressive action by Japan seemed to justify New Zealand fears. In 1931 Japanese troops occupied Manchuria, which became a

Japanese puppet state, Manchuquo. Japanese forces fought Chinese near Shanghai in the following year, and in 1933 Japan walked out of the League of Nations after its actions were condemned by the world body. Outright but undeclared war between Japan and China followed in 1937, demonstrating Japan's aggressive ambitions but for the time being allaying concerns in the South Pacific. Japan, it seemed, had bitten off more than it could chew—a feeling that seemed confirmed when Japan, in September 1939, refrained from standing alongside its ally, Nazi Germany, when war began in Europe.

In the early part of the Second World War, New Zealand's attention focused on the Middle East, to which it dispatched an expeditionary force in early 1940. Other New Zealanders were sent to Europe to serve with the Royal Navy and the Royal Air Force; they were soon to be found serving in warships and squadrons in every theatre of the war.

Kallang airbase, Singapore. Ray Ansdell collection

Some of these units were sent to the Pacific, especially to the main British outposts in the region, Hong Kong and Singapore. In 1940, 10 yachtsmen, specially recruited in New Zealand, arrived at Singapore to man small naval craft (another 22 would be sent in 1941). A few expatriate New Zealanders joined local defence battalions in Malaya and Hong Kong. Although New Zealand—unlike Australia—sent no ground forces to Singapore, it did dispatch about 400 RNZAF personnel in 1941. Most of these men were members of an aerodrome construction squadron which built several airfields in southern Malaya. One of those whose stories are related below, Bill Mitchell, was among a handful of groundcrew sent to Singapore at this time. They were joined in October 1941 by the first fighter squadron raised in New Zealand. Although commanded by a Battle of Britain veteran, this unit comprised mainly men who were straight out of training schools. Their preparations for combat were hindered by the tropical conditions and the lack of equipment.

The New Zealanders were amazed by the atmosphere in Singapore. 'It was almost like a peacetime station,' Bill Mitchell recalls; 'there was no urgency about anything.' This complacency seemed all the more difficult to understand as the international outlook darkened. With an increasingly assertive United States demanding Japanese withdrawal from China and Indo-China (into which Japan had sent forces in 1940–41 following France's defeat by Germany), Japan was confronted with a dilemma. To accede to American demands—made more pressing by the imposition of an oil embargo—would destroy Japan's hopes of carving out for itself an economic sphere in the western Pacific and Southeast Asia. But to ignore them would mean war with a power possessing a more powerful navy and huge latent strength, a war in which victory would be uncertain. The oil embargo added urgency to the decision: if it was to fight, Japan must do so before its oil reserves dwindled below those necessary for mounting a campaign.

Japan's rulers opted for war. While continuing diplomatic negotiations, its war planners began preparing for hostilities. Japan would fight not only the United States, but also the British—another superior naval power—and the Dutch. Japanese forces would land in southern Thailand and Malaya and move down the peninsula to neutralise the base at Singapore and occupy the Dutch East Indies (now Indonesia), which was rich in the desperately needed oil. In effect, Japan aimed to supplant the Southeast Asian empires of the British, Dutch and Americans (who had ruled the Philippines since taking them from Spain in 1898).

DEFEAT

THE MAN CHARGED WITH STRIKING Japan's blow against the United States, Commander-in-Chief of the Combined Fleet Admiral Isoroku Yamamoto, did so with mixed feelings. In the lead-up to war, he warned that 'we can run wild for six months or a year, but after that I have utterly no confidence'. His prediction proved remarkably accurate. On what US President Franklin D. Roosevelt would describe as 'a date which will live in infamy', 7 December 1941 (before dawn on 8 December, New Zealand time), Japan shocked the world. Carrier-borne warplanes swooped down on 'battleship row' in Pearl Harbor, on the Hawaiian island of Oahu, sinking or badly damaging seven of the nine battleships there. But, fatally for Japan, it was not a complete annihilation: the US fleet's three aircraft carriers were absent from the base at the crucial moment, leaving a core on which to rebuild US seapower.

Meanwhile, as planned, Japanese troops had landed in southern Thailand before the first bombs fell at Pearl Harbor. Later in the day Japanese aircraft from Indo-China appeared over Singapore. While their troops battled mainly Indian soldiers in northern Malaya, Japanese aircraft destroyed the two British capital ships that had been sent to Singapore in a desperate bid to deter the Japanese government from going to war—a far cry from the fleet envisaged in earlier British plans for war with Japan. The sinking of the new battleship HMS *Prince of Wales* and the battlecruiser HMS *Repulse* off the coast of Malaya on 10 December cast a pall over the whole Commonwealth. That these mighty ships had succumbed so easily came as a shock, not least because most New Zealanders, like other Westerners, had little respect for

Japanese fighting qualities. Among the crews of these ships were a number of New Zealanders. Two who were lost were almost certainly the first of their countrymen to die in battle with Japan. They were among the approximately 75 New Zealand seamen and airmen who lost their lives during the Malayan campaign and in the fall of Hong Kong.

Driving down the Malay peninsula, the Japanese had Singapore under siege by the end of January 1942. As they approached, New Zealand's aerodrome constructors blew up their newly completed airfields and pulled back to the island. As the threat to the vital base grew, New Zealand pilots fought valiantly

Damaged buildings and fires on the Singapore waterfront, 16 February 1942, the day after the British surrender. Australian War Memorial, Neg. 127904

against long odds, their Buffalo Brewster aircraft no match for the Japanese Zeros they confronted. Air raids drastically reduced their aircraft, quickly accounting for the modern Hurricane fighters that arrived in early January. Eventually the survivors withdrew to the Dutch East Indies. The fall of Singapore on 15 February 1942 was the greatest British military defeat since the surrender at Yorktown in 1781 that had effectively decided the American War of Independence. More than 130,000 troops laid down their arms. The Japanese wasted little time in thrusting into the Dutch East Indies, where they captured some of the New Zealanders who had managed to escape from Singapore, including Ian Newlands, whose story is told in this book. On 19 February, carrier-borne aircraft mounted a heavy raid on Darwin, killing several hundred people and causing extensive damage. This was the first of many air raids on Australia.

Numerous New Zealanders remained in action after Singapore's fall. Some helped man RAF squadrons that tried to halt the Japanese in Burma. Seamen serving in British warships faced great danger as Japanese forces prevailed in a series of actions in Dutch East Indies waters. New Zealand's own cruisers, HMNZS *Achilles* and *Leander*, formed part of a Suva-based Anzac Squadron which operated in the South Pacific, where the Japanese had now appeared, seizing most of the Solomon Islands. To the northeast, they had also moved into the western part of the Gilbert Islands, where they captured eight New Zealand

A New Zealand camp in Fiji. ATL, Jim Henderson Collection, F-116447-1/2

coastwatchers—men who had been sent north in the previous year to undertake the lonely task of observing Japanese movements in the islands. Taken to Tokyo in January 1942, they were the first New Zealand prisoners of the Japanese to arrive in the Japanese capital. Although they faced a long period of captivity, they were fortunate. When the Japanese occupied the rest of the group later in the year they rounded up 17 New Zealanders and beheaded them, with five others, at Tarawa after an American air raid. This was the worst atrocity involving New Zealanders during the war.

New Zealand troops in Fiji braced themselves for action in early 1942. The first of them had arrived in the islands in 1940 as members of 8 Infantry Brigade. They had toiled hard with inadequate equipment to improve the defences, building coastal gun emplacements and preparing facilities for camps. Harry Bioletti was one of those who became involved in the defence of Fiji when his battalion was deployed there to replace one of the brigade's units. A small number of New Zealand officers and NCOs sent to Tonga to organise and train the Tongan Defence Force would be followed later by personnel to man coast defence guns installed at Nuku'alofa.

In November 1941, the New Zealand government had agreed to build three airfields in the Fijian islands for the United States, which was anxious to create a southern Pacific route to the Philippines. A thousand men recruited from the Public Works Department were soon hard at work on this project, which they completed ahead of schedule. When Japan entered the war, another brigade, the 14th, was hastily dispatched to Fiji to bolster the defences. Other New Zealanders, officers and NCOs, served with the Fiji military forces. Their numbers grew steadily to 800 in August 1943—about 10 per cent of the force—and some went into action with Fijian units in the Solomons.

In New Zealand itself, anti-invasion defences were being thrown up and home defence forces mobilised to man them. The turn of events had led some to ask whether New Zealand's most effective military unit, 2 Division, which had been in hard action against Axis forces in North Africa when Japan struck, should be brought home to face the enemy at the gates. This seemed all the more necessary when it became apparent that two of the three Australian divisions in the Middle East were being redeployed to the Pacific. A myth has developed that immediately after Pearl Harbor Australia demanded the return of its troops while the more compliant New Zealand deferred to the British government in leaving its

Members of the Somme Battalion of the Home Guard on a route march around Wellington harbour from Petone to Eastbourne. ATL, John Pascoe Collection, F-2026-1/4

division in Egypt. In fact, Australia's deployment was made as a result of a British request, not an Australian demand—although controversy arose while the troops were en route when Australia rejected British suggestions that the troops be landed in Burma, insisting that they return to Australia for home defence. By the time this redeployment was completed and shipping became available for the possible movement of New Zealand troops, the situation had deteriorated to such an extent that any sea movement in the Indian Ocean would have been very dangerous because of marauding Japanese warships. A safer alternative existed: American troops could be sent to New Zealand. The first arrived in June 1942.

Ironically, given the effort being made to bolster home defences, the first Japanese incursion into New Zealand waters went unchallenged. On 8 March 1942 the submarine *I-25* passed through Cook Strait. It launched a small seaplane, which flew around Wellington harbour looking for American warships. Some heard the plane, but the fact that it was Japanese was not revealed until after the war. The submarine repeated the exercise at Auckland shortly afterwards, before heading north towards Fiji.

RECOVERY

THE STARTLING SUCCESS of Japan's onslaught left it with a conundrum: what should it do next? Most of its troops were still heavily engaged in China; others were pressing the remnants of British forces in Burma back towards India. It quickly became apparent that for the time being there were insufficient military units available for an invasion of Australia. The Japanese high command decided therefore to cut off Australia and New Zealand while they concentrated on the most pressing task—bringing the reviving US Navy to battle and decisively defeating it. Proponents of this approach had their case boosted when on 18 April 1942 American bombers launched from a US carrier attacked Tokyo and other targets—the famous Doolittle raid, which did little physical damage but greatly boosted Allied morale. Japan's immediate goal in the South Pacific was to capture the whole of Papua New Guinea and the island groups to its east, including Fiji and Samoa. As the first step, a seaborne force would capture Port Moresby.

Resolute action by the US Navy confounded Japan's intentions. Forewarned by signals intelligence—codebreakers had successfully penetrated Japanese naval codes—Nimitz sent two of his precious aircraft carriers to the South Pacific. On 7 May they intercepted the Japanese force heading for Port Moresby in the Coral Sea. The ensuing battle broke new ground in naval warfare: for the first time fleets fought an action without coming within sight of each other, using aircraft rather than big guns. Both sides suffered damage, but the Japanese turned back. Their attempt to take Port Moresby by sea was foiled, and Japanese forces would subsequently advance overland, only to be halted and eventually driven back by Australian forces on the infamous Kokoda Trail. The Battle of the Coral Sea drastically affected Japanese plans in the area, leading eventually to the cancellation of the intended operations against Fiji and other islands. Many in New Zealand and Australia, unaware that Japan had never planned to invade them, firmly believed that the Battle of the Coral Sea halted an inexorable Japanese advance towards them.

The battle that actually determined whether or not New Zealand would be invaded at some future point occurred a month later, far to the north, off Midway Island. This encounter was deliberately sought by the Japanese as a means of completing the destruction of American naval power. A huge armada bore down on Midway, an outlier of the Hawaiian Islands; the aim was to lure the US fleet into the area and pounce on it. Again forewarned by the codebreakers, Nimitz was able to ambush the enemy and inflict decisive damage. The outcome completely changed the strategic picture, with the US Navy left superior to Japan in the aircraft carriers that were confirmed to be the main elements of naval power. The initiative had been wrenched away from Tokyo.

This victory set the stage for New Zealand's involvement in the struggle against the Japanese in the South Pacific. The Americans wasted no time in preparing to launch a counteroffensive against the Japanese forces in the Solomon Islands. US Marines who had briefly sojourned at McKays Crossing, near Paekakariki, landed on the island of Guadalcanal on 7 August, their immediate objective being the seizure of an airfield the Japanese had built (soon renamed Henderson Field). The Japanese response was vigorous. As the fighting intensified, both sides rapidly built up their forces on the island. Vicious battles, some on a major scale, erupted in the surrounding waters as the Americans tried to prevent Japanese naval forces—the 'Tokyo Express'—from bringing in reinforcements. Both sides lost heavily. It would be four months before the Americans gained the upper hand on the island. The surviving Japanese were eventually evacuated by their naval forces.

New Zealand was a forward base for this effort. As well as preparing for battle in camps around Auckland and at Paekakariki, Americans came back to New Zealand from the islands for rest, recuperation, and recovery from wounds or illnesses. Some 800 Japanese prisoners of war were brought from the Solomons to a camp established near Featherston. Many were deeply depressed by the dishonour of

Wrecked Japanese troop carrier, Lunga, Guadalcanal, 1943. Thomas White collection

being in captivity, a feeling that underlay a bloody incident on 25 February 1943. Forty-eight of the prisoners were killed or wounded by guards after a suicidal charge by the Japanese. A soldier killed by a ricochet has the dubious distinction of being the only New Zealander to lose his life because of enemy action on New Zealand soil. New Zealand also contributed to the American effort in the Solomons by providing food and other supplies.

The first New Zealand servicemen involved in the Solomons campaign were seamen. After escorting troop and supply ships from the United States to the South Pacific, first *Leander* (soon recalled because of hull damage) and then *Achilles* joined American naval forces near Guadalcanal. The latter's service in the theatre was cut short on 5 January 1943 by a bomb that killed 13 crewmen. Even before the island was secured, Hudson bombers of 3 Squadron, which had been deployed to Espiritu Santo in the New Hebrides (now Vanuatu) in October 1942, arrived at Henderson Field. From November 1942 they mounted reconnaissance flights throughout the Solomons. This presence was augmented when the Royal New Zealand Navy's 25th Minesweeping Flotilla, comprising the corvettes HMNZS *Moa*, *Kiwi*, *Tui*, and *Matai*, arrived in the following month and began nightly patrols from a base at nearby Tulagi. They soon made their presence felt. On the night of 29–30 January 1943, *Kiwi* and *Moa* located and forced to the surface the Japanese submarine *I-1*. The New Zealand corvettes prevailed over their much larger opponent in a furious fight at close quarters, with *Kiwi* ramming the submarine and forcing it aground.

Meanwhile, New Zealand had been preparing a land force for service in the islands. Following its withdrawal from Fiji in mid-1942, 3 Division had been training for such service under the command of Major-General H.E. Barrowclough, a citizen-soldier who was also appointed commander of 2NZEF in the Pacific. In November 1942 it began deploying to New Caledonia, where it relieved American troops to allow them to join the battle on Guadalcanal. Base facilities were established on the island, work began on a base hospital, and training continued. The division was for the time being under-strength because two battalions had been detached to garrison Tonga and Norfolk Island in October 1942. On the latter

Major-General Harold Barrowclough (left) with the US Military Attaché for New Zealand, John H. Nankivell, in New Caledonia. ATL, War History Collection, WH-0745

island, Peter Renshaw was one of the New Zealanders who endured the rather humdrum existence of a garrison soldier, feeling frustrated as 'There was nothing much to do. . . . We felt we were just sitting in the backwater . . . .' The New Zealand battalion at Tonga served under American command, the United States having assumed responsibility for the island (and Fiji) earlier in the year. An RNZAF fighter squadron was also sent to the group. The Tongan deployment was undertaken to free more American units to go forward to the Solomons.

For the troops in all three locations (as earlier in Fiji), boredom was a major problem. Even later, when the troops went into action in the Solomons, there would be long periods of garrison duty. The stimulation of settling into a new location soon wore off. The stories in this book indicate the varied ways in which the men tried to keep themselves occupied. Card games whiled away many an off-duty hour, and gambling was common. Reading and letter-writing were popular pastimes, and there were opportunities to view movies on open-air screens. Ralph Williams started a band, and others enjoyed

Kiwi soldiers take part in a woodchopping competition, New Caledonia, 1943. ATL, War History Collection, F–20402-1/4

sing-along sessions. Some men showed enterprise by creating a whisky-still in the jungle. Others made souvenirs to sell to Americans. Collecting butterflies was popular among some on Bougainville. At Jacquinot Bay on New Britain, airmen fashioned makeshift yachts. Occasional sports meetings were another enjoyable break from routine. In Fiji, there had been rugby against barefooted locals. A rugby competition was organised in New Caledonia, and men also tried American sports such as baseball. Swimming was popular, although sometimes hindered by sea snakes and jellyfish.

While Barrowclough's men on New Caledonia and elsewhere chafed at their relative inactivity, a small number of New Zealand soldiers were in action against the enemy on Guadalcanal. Officers and NCOs serving with a Fijian commando unit, they were sent to the island in December 1942 and engaged in scouting missions behind Japanese lines. Another Fijian unit with substantial New Zealand representation replaced these men in early 1943: 1 Commando Fiji Guerillas became part of the South Sea Scouts, which included contingents of Tongans and Solomon Islanders. The scouts played an active role in New Georgia, which the Americans invaded in June 1943 as the next stage in their drive north. Fighting bogged down, and it took several months to secure the airstrip at Munda.

As at Guadalcanal, the waters around New Georgia were the scene of sudden, desperate naval clashes as the 'Tokyo Express' sought to reinforce and replenish the defenders. One such action, on the night of 12–13 July 1943, almost put paid to *Leander*, as James Murphy recounts. A chief petty officer in the forward engine room, he heard 'an almighty muffled bang' and the ship 'shook as though there was a severe earthquake'. Hit by a torpedo, *Leander* was saved from sinking only by the strenuous efforts of her crew. Twenty-eight men lost their lives, and Murphy recalls the terrible smell of burnt human remains that permeated parts of the ship. This disaster spelt the end of the involvement of New Zealand cruisers in the Solomons fighting. *Leander* went to the United States for repairs and never returned to the RNZN. The New Zealand naval presence was sustained by the four corvettes of the minesweeping flotilla (HMNZS *Gale* had replaced *Kiwi*). After *Moa* was sunk by a bomb during a Japanese raid on Tulagi harbour on 7 April 1943 with the loss of five crewmen, her place had been taken by HMNZS *Breeze*. *Tui* helped to sink the submarine *I-17* between New Caledonia and Espiritu Santo in August 1943.

As the fighting proceeded, New Zealand's presence in the theatre was expanded. In April 1943 the fighter squadron at Tonga (15 Squadron) was redeployed to the Solomons; it began operating from an airstrip on Guadalcanal. From September another squadron would join it. This fighter deployment was maintained by a revolving deployment from Espiritu Santo and New Zealand. Each squadron—five

*Among those admiring the
scoreboard of the RNZAF
Fighter Wing in New Georgia
are the Governor-General,
Sir Cyril Newall (second from
right) and Major-General
Barrowclough (right).*
ATL, Evatt Collection,
F-106437-1/2

were involved, numbered 14 to 18—deployed to Espiritu Santo for six weeks, then went forward into the operational area for six weeks before being withdrawn to New Zealand to rest, its place taken by another from Espiritu Santo. Pilots thus had limited time in the forward area, although some would do as many as six tours during the course of the campaign. Their groundcrews were not so lucky, having to endure the heat and monotony of island life for a year before being relieved.

The pilots, flying Kittyhawks, battled Japanese air forces in the skies over the Solomons. Dogfights were common as they intercepted Japanese bombing raids, or escorted bombers on raids against Japanese positions on New Georgia, and in due course Bougainville and New Britain. In these air battles, Japanese air strength was whittled down by the New Zealand and American pilots. New Zealand airmen shot down more than 100 Japanese aircraft, the last in February 1944. By this time the Allies had established complete air supremacy in the area. The Japanese responded by pulling the remnants of their air forces in the Solomons back to Truk, the Japanese bastion far to the north in the eastern Caroline Islands.

After some doubts about whether it would ever be used in action, 3 Division finally got its chance, practising a landing in the New Hebrides before going ashore on Guadalcanal in August. Several of the men interviewed for this book recalled their shock at the appearance of parts of the island. The intensity of the shelling had stripped trees of their leaves or snapped their trunks. In this battered landscape they continued training for their first task, on Vella Lavella, where Americans had landed in the previous month. The New Zealanders would take over from them and complete the destruction of Japanese forces on the island. After landing on Vella Lavella on 18 September, troops of 14 Brigade experienced for the first time the horrors of jungle warfare, seeking out an elusive enemy who, they were uncomfortably aware, could be unseen just feet from them. The danger of being shot by a sniper or cut down in an ambush was ever present. Sharp little actions took a steady toll. By the time the surviving Japanese evacuated the island on 30 September, 32 New Zealanders had lost their lives. In the months that followed, the troops once more endured the monotony of garrison duty. As in New Caledonia, they tried to make themselves as comfortable as possible.

The division was next charged with making an opposed landing in the Treasury Islands, mainly to secure a site for radar facilities needed for the much larger landing being planned for Bougainville soon afterwards. The landing by 8 Brigade on Mono Island on 27 October 1943 was the first amphibious

New Zealand troops soon after arriving at Guadalcanal, 1943. LCIs can be seen in the background. ATL, War History Collection, WH-0710

The path to the beach at Soanatalu, Mono Island. ATL, War History Collection, F-20465-1/4

operation by New Zealand forces since Gallipoli. As the troops went ashore, New Zealand fighter pilots, now based at Ondonga in New Georgia, were among those covering them overhead. The troops landed without serious opposition and quickly dealt with the island's defenders. A small force that had landed on the north coast, where the radar would be located facing Bougainville, had some anxious moments when they were strongly attacked by Japanese from the south. Almost from the moment the troops were ashore, engineers were hard at work building facilities, including an airfield on Stirling Island, near Mono. In the fortnight it took to complete the operation, 40 New Zealanders were killed.

Within days American forces had stormed ashore on Bougainville and seized an enclave around Empress Augusta Bay. The Marines who carried out this operation on 1 November had come from New Zealand, where they had been camped near Auckland for six months. Here, too, the engineers wasted little time in constructing airfields (Piva and Torokina) from which Allied squadrons were soon operating, among them New Zealand's fighter squadrons. In March 1944 the Japanese made a determined attempt to overrun the enclave. Two New Zealand dive-bomber squadrons which arrived at this time bombed attacking Japanese troops within sight of their airfield. Groundcrewman Bill Mitchell, who was now based at Piva, found himself in the third defence line, but the Japanese advance was halted before he was required to take up his weapon. Once again New Zealanders took part in the ground fighting as members of Fijian units used for reconnaissance behind enemy lines.

Early in 1944 the New Zealanders made yet another landing. Their target this time was the Green Islands, close to the Japanese base at Rabaul, the main objective of Nimitz's forces in the Solomons and those fighting eastwards in New Guinea under General MacArthur. Harry Bioletti was in a force that landed on the main island in the group, Nissan, shortly before the main landing. He recalls that the purpose of this was 'reconnaissance to see what was going on up there and how many Japs were there'. The main landing, on 15 February, easily secured the island, which was rapidly transformed into an airbase from which the fighter-bomber squadrons attacked Rabaul.

The Nissan action proved to be 3 Division's swansong, however, for it soon afterwards fell victim to New Zealand's

Men of a mortar section seek a position for their weapons, Nissan Island.
Harry Bioletti collection

increasing manpower problems. Faced with the problem of sustaining 2 Division in Italy, 3 Division in the Solomons, and farm production in New Zealand, the government opted to run down 3 Division. Barrowclough's disappointed men began pulling back from their island outposts to New Caledonia. Hopes that the division might yet be saved were soon dashed. The men were transported back to New Zealand in August 1944, and the division was disbanded soon afterwards. New Zealand's effort in the Solomons was henceforth sustained by its seamen and airmen. The former were augmented by two flotillas of Fairmile motor launches that were deployed in March 1944. These 12 small craft carried out a range of tasks as far north as the Admiralty Islands, without Japanese opposition. They and the minesweeping flotilla continued to operate in the islands until June 1945.

Nissan became a familiar place for the pilots who constituted the main element of New Zealand's effort in the Solomons. Their numbers grew steadily, and more than 8000 airmen were serving in the islands by early 1945. The administrative framework also burgeoned. The RNZAF's main base was at Espiritu Santo; from March 1943 New Zealand's air effort had been controlled by 1 (Islands) Group, which established its headquarters on Guadalcanal. By February 1944 the group included eight squadrons.

In addition to the bomber-reconnaissance and fighter-bomber squadrons, now flying Venturas and Corsairs respectively, flying-boat squadrons (operating mainly Catalinas) played a key role in recovering downed airmen—the so-called Dumbo patrols—and transport squadrons equipped mainly with Dakotas maintained the link with New Zealand. Eventually 15 squadrons would form part of the redesignated New Zealand Air Task Force, operating from bases in the northern Solomons and Jacquinot Bay on New Britain. Richard Mapp arrived at the latter in May 1945.

Operations from early 1944 were confined to bombing Rabaul and its surrounds and the areas of Bougainville still held by the Japanese, who were now being fought by Australian troops. These operations against an enemy which no longer had any ability to mount attacks continued until the end of the war. Lives were lost in fighting that no longer had much relevance to the defeat of Japan. The airmen regularly faced the dangers of flak over Rabaul and to a lesser extent over parts of Bougainville, and at other times endured long, monotonous patrols in uncomfortably hot cockpits. Engine failure and other equipment malfunctions took a steady toll of lives. Climatic conditions could also be lethal. Doug Benge remembers being confronted by a storm while returning from a mission. 'It's like flying alongside a big black wall.' He had to wait for it to pass before heading into his base. Others were less fortunate. It was the elements rather than the Japanese that caused the RNZAF's blackest day of the campaign, 15 January 1945. When a tropical storm disoriented pilots returning from a mission to protect a colleague who had been shot down and was floating in Rabaul harbour, seven lost their lives when they crashed or collided in the murk at or near Nissan. (The RNZAF was to suffer an even blacker day three weeks after war ended, when a Dakota transport with 20 on board disappeared without trace en route from Espiritu Santo to New Zealand.)

VICTORY

EVEN AS NEW ZEALAND TROOPS LANDED on Mono in November 1943, a significant change was taking place that would very shortly render the Solomons area a backwater. Nimitz's forces prepared to launch a massive offensive through the central Pacific. The first blow was the landing of Marines (again from New Zealand) on Tarawa in the Gilbert Islands. This was the first in a series of island-hopping operations that took the American forces ever closer to Japan. No New Zealand units took part in this drive, but a few radar specialists were present, including Alan Roberts, whose involvement ended when he was wounded at Peleliu in the Palau group. Meanwhile, another prong of the American thrust was provided by MacArthur's forces, which invaded the Philippines. When the Japanese tried to counter this operation, the ensuing Battle of Leyte Gulf completed the destruction of their naval power. Invasions of Okinawa and Iwo Jima followed. Fanatical resistance, including kamikaze attacks on Allied warships, could not prevent the Americans taking these islands,

The imprint of a Japanese kamikaze aircraft on the side of HMS Sussex, *which was not damaged by the impact.* Australian War Memorial, Neg. P02690.001

which provided bases from which US bombers devastated the flammable Japanese cities.

With Japanese seapower now virtually non-existent, huge Allied naval task forces ranged the waters of the Japanese home islands, bombarding coastal installations. New Zealand played a part in these final operations. Many New Zealand seamen were serving in vessels of the British fleet which took part. There was substantial representation in the Fleet Air Arm crews, who had already made their presence felt while the fleet was making its way east, taking part in a major air raid on Japanese oil installations in Sumatra. (Two New Zealand airmen shot down and captured in this operation were beheaded in Singapore only days before the end of the war.) New Zealand also sent its own vessels to serve with the fleet. The cruisers *Achilles* and *Gambia*, which had replaced *Leander*, served with the British Pacific Fleet, as did the corvette HMNZS *Arbutus*. The hospital ship HMNZHS *Maunganui* joined the fleet train. Pita Tauwhare, whose recollections are included in this collection, was a seaman boy on *Achilles*, while John McKay served on the aircraft carriers HMS *Illustrious* and *Formidable*. He was wounded on the latter when a kamikaze pilot crashed his plane on the flight deck. Thomas White was nearby on the destroyer HMS *Quilliam*, which had tried to shoot down the Japanese plane. Soon afterwards *Quilliam* had the misfortune to collide with another aircraft carrier.

These operations overshadowed fighting on the western periphery of the Japanese Empire in which numerous New Zealanders were also involved—the campaign to drive the Japanese out of Burma. Seventy New Zealand engineer officers made available to the Indian Army after 1942 helped to sustain the communications on which the British 14th Army depended. More than 300 New Zealand airmen made their mark with the RAF squadrons supporting the troops. Further east, a handful took part in covert operations against the enemy in Borneo as members of the so-called Z Special Unit. Plans were in train for an RNZAF task force to deploy to this area as well.

While Allied naval and air forces battered the Japanese homeland virtually at will, ending the war seemed to require an invasion that was viewed with foreboding. The fanatical enemy resistance on Iwo

General Douglas MacArthur signs the peace terms aboard USS Missouri, *September 1945. New Zealand's Air Vice-Marshal Leonard Isitt is fourth from left.* Royal New Zealand Navy Museum, AAI 0114

Jima and Okinawa indicated the perils of such an operation. The New Zealand government agreed that New Zealand would provide a two-brigade force to take part. Plans were in train to send several 'New Zealand' squadrons in the RAF to the east, and many other New Zealand airmen would no doubt have taken part in ordinary RAF squadrons. But these decisions were overtaken by events. On 6 August an American bomber dropped an atomic bomb on Hiroshima. This fearsome new weapon, in the development of which a handful of New Zealand scientists took part, had been tested in the Utah desert just three weeks earlier. It was used in an attempt to bring the war to a speedy conclusion, saving lives by obviating the need for an invasion and, hopefully, forestalling Soviet plans to enter the war. This latter hope was dashed, however, when Soviet forces invaded Manchuria on 8 August, quickly shattering the Japanese army there. Next day a second atom bomb destroyed the city of Nagasaki. More than 100,000 people were killed as a result of the bombs. At this point the Japanese capitulated, the Emperor, speaking directly to his people for the first time, telling them that they would have to endure the unendurable.

Japan formally surrendered on 2 September, its representatives boarding the battleship USS *Missouri* in Tokyo Bay to sign the instrument of surrender. New Zealand's cruiser *Gambia* was among the 400 Allied warships crowded into the bay. Air Vice-Marshal Leonard Isitt signed the document on New Zealand's behalf, bringing to an end six years of war. Because of the nature of New Zealand's war effort, the Pacific War toll had proved mercifully light. New Zealand lost just over 700 soldiers, sailors, and airmen in the struggle with Japan (about 6 per cent of its total fatal casualties). About 200 men and women endured imprisonment in Japanese camps, roughly half of them civilians. In 1946 New Zealand provided an infantry brigade group and an air force squadron to the Commonwealth forces that helped to occupy Japan, a commitment that continued until 1948.

REFLECTIONS

THE SOLOMONS CAMPAIGN was the closest to New Zealand of all its overseas efforts. The fact that it was fought on a smaller scale than the war in Europe was apparent to the many former 3 Division personnel who eventually found themselves fighting in Italy after being sent as reinforcements. There was a tendency among 2 Division personnel to belittle the service of these men. It was galling to Pacific War veterans to find that this attitude was also shared by many at home. 'We were branded as

Men of 14 Brigade with a boat abandoned by Japanese troops, Vella Lavella. ATL, War History Collection, WH-0215

coconut bombers as distinct from the men of steel in the desert,' Noel Rosoman recalls. 'We were either coconut bombers or banana pickers.' They believed that their service had not been given the credit it was due, that it had been overshadowed by the intense public interest in Freyberg's division fighting against the Germans. The interviews reproduced in this book reveal men who did their duty quietly and efficiently. When finally given the opportunity, the soldiers among them demonstrated considerable skill in fighting in an environment entirely different from that in which New Zealanders had operated in the past. In this respect, they upheld the New Zealand military tradition in fine fashion. They trained hard, and it was no discredit to them that their efforts were cut short by political decisions in Wellington. The seamen and airmen, of course, did not suffer from this constraint. Some were involved in taking the surrender of Japanese still in island outposts throughout the southwest Pacific in August 1945.

Despite the relative lack of recognition, most of those whose stories are told here are positive about their involvement. 'It was a marvellous experience and it took you to places that you'd never go,' Bill Mitchell notes. They were proud to have served in a theatre close to their homeland, and to feel that they were contributing directly to its defence. 'We didn't mind scrapping in the Pacific, it was nearer home,' Jim Murphy explains. 'It [the war] was a local thing, whereas before that it was a long way away from home.' Ralph Williams may speak for all those represented in this book when he states that 'The

N.H. Bonsell on amphibious training with the unit dog, Pooch. ATL, War History Collection, WH-0155

war never did me any harm. I was so grateful and lucky to come out unscathed.'

Racial stereotypes were employed during the Pacific War, and the New Zealanders who took part shared many of the attitudes prevalent at the time among their allies. They had relatively little contact with the enemy, but they feared them because of their reputation for committing atrocities and their suicidal bent when cornered. The sight of Japanese prisoners did little to alter such attitudes, although it did sometimes undermine stereotypes about Japanese generally. When, after the capitulation, some New Zealand prisoners returned from Japanese camps in an emaciated state, there was revulsion against the Japanese among the public. (Ironically, despite the fact that New Zealand treated its prisoners incomparably better than the Japanese did, more Japanese had died in New Zealand hands than New Zealanders in Japanese camps because of the Featherston affray.) Although New Zealand had relatively few returning prisoners, many Australians had been in Japanese hands, and a shocking 8000 of them had died. The bitter hatred that revelations of the treatment of Allied prisoners engendered would persist long after the war. Sixty years later, some of the men interviewed for this book no longer hold any feelings of resentment towards the Japanese, but others admit to still hating them.

New Zealanders who took part in the war in the Pacific were witnesses to a stupendous build-up of American power. Many among the troops, and the people back home, believed that the United States had saved New Zealand from invasion in 1942. There was admiration mixed with some bemusement at the way in which Americans went about the business of war, not least in regard to the material comforts that ordinary US servicemen enjoyed. New Zealanders' friendly interactions with Americans, both at home and in the islands, began to break down the overwhelmingly British-oriented culture of the country. Although for good strategic reasons New Zealand made its main effort in the European theatre, the Pacific War would prove to be more important to it in the long run. The soldiers, sailors, and airmen who participated did so in part to stake New Zealand's claim to a say in the settlement that would follow the war. It was clear that the United States—the Pacific's superpower—would dominate that settlement, and the fact that New Zealanders and Americans had stood shoulder-to-shoulder redounded to New Zealand's advantage. In 1951, with Australia, it would enter an alliance with the United States in a reassertion of the common interests that had underlain their co-operation in the Pacific War.

FURTHER READING

For a comprehensive account of New Zealand's involvement in the Pacific War, see the following official histories produced by the War History Branch of the Department of Internal Affairs: O.A. Gillespie, *The Pacific* (1952); Squadron-Leader J.M.S. Ross, *Royal New Zealand Air Force* (1955); S.D. Waters, *Royal New Zealand Navy* (1956); and Wing Commander H.L. Thompson, *New Zealanders with the Royal Air Force*, Volume III (1959). The official histories can also be found online at http://www.nzetc.org/projects/wh2/index.html. A 13-volume series of semi-official histories edited by O.A. Gillespie tells the story of 3 Division, while the role of New Zealanders who served in Fijian forces is covered in both Gillespie's official history and Colin R. Larsen, *Pacific Commandos: New Zealanders and Fijians in Action: A History of Southern Independent Commando and First Commando Fiji Guerrillas* (1946). The activities of coastwatchers are described in D.O.W. Hall, *Coastwatchers* (1951). On the fate of prisoners of war, see: W.W. Mason, *Prisoners of War* (1954); D.O.W. Hall, *Prisoners of Japan* (1949); and Megan Hutching (ed.), *Inside Stories: New Zealand Prisoners of War Remember* (2002). On the efforts of New Zealand's radar personnel, see Ross Galbreath, 'Dr Marsden and Admiral Halsey: New Zealand Radar Scientists in the Pacific War', in John Crawford (ed.), *Kia Kaha: New Zealand in the Second World War* (2002). On Z Special Force, see Gabrielle McDonald, *New Zealand's Secret Heroes: Don Stott and the 'Z' Special Unit* (1991). For the overall context of the campaign, see Ian McGibbon, *New Zealand and the Second World War: The People, the Battles and the Legacy* (2004). Short accounts are provided in John Crawford, *New Zealand's Pacific Frontline: Guadalcanal–Solomon Islands Campaign 1942–45* (1992) and Matthew Wright, *Pacific War: New Zealand and Japan 1941–45* (2003). Personal memoirs of soldiers include T.E. Dorman, *The Green War* (1997). There are also a number of recollections by pilots, including: Alex Horn, *Wings Over the Pacific: The RNZAF in the Pacific Air War* (1992); Bryan Cox, *Too Young to Die: The Story of a New Zealand Fighter Pilot in the Pacific War* (1987); Keith Mulligan, *Kittyhawks and Coconuts* (1995); and Sir Frank Holmes, *Jungle Bomber: With Avengers and Corsairs in the Solomons* (2004). Bryan Cox's *Pacific Scrapbook 1943–1947: A Pictorial History of a Young New Zealand Corsair Pilot in the Pacific and Japan and of Allied Co-operation in the Pacific War* (1997) provides a pictorial account of the RNZAF's efforts in the Solomons campaign.

'EVERYBODY BECAME PRISONER OF WAR'

IAN NEWLANDS, NZ404927,
SERGEANT PILOT,
ROYAL NEW ZEALAND AIR FORCE

Ian Newlands, the son of a Presbyterian minister and his wife, grew up in Otago and Southland. He was studying mathematics and physics at Canterbury University College when war was declared in 1939. He enlisted in the air force and went into camp in December 1940. After learning to fly at Harewood, Ian was sent to Canada on the Empire Air Training Scheme and trained at Dunnville in Ontario on Yale and Harvard aircraft. He spent some time in Iceland en route to England, where he joined 43 Squadron. In October 1941 he was posted to 232 Squadron and went, via Khartoum in Sudan, to Java on board HMS Indomitable. *In February 1942 the squadron was posted to Kallang aerodrome, Singapore. On 11 February, three days after the Japanese landed, he was sent to Seletar airfield in the north of the island to pick up a repaired plane to fly back to Java.*

IT WAS PRETTY SCARY, we had our revolvers out the window all the time. We stopped two Sikh guards, and they said go ahead. My plane started up right away and I said, 'We don't want to stick around with the motor going because the Japanese will hear me across the strait and start shelling', so I just took off. I thought, While I'm up I will see if I can find that observation balloon that they've got over there, so I flew up and down on the enemy side of the strait. Couldn't see the balloon, so I just strafed the jungle and along the shore, and turned back for home. I thought, I'm going to go back and get a bit of breakfast now. I've done a good day's work, and I'll go back to the 'drome after that. When I got there there wasn't a plane left. They'd all gone, left us. They'd left us without any planes

Previous page: *The aftermath of a Japanese attack on Singapore, December 1941.* Australian War Memorial, Neg. 010840
Above: *Ian Newlands in late 1945.* Ian Newlands collection

Above: *Ian Newlands (left) at Harewood, 1941.*
Ian Newlands collection

Left: *Burning wreckage on the airfield after a Japanese air raid. This is probably RAF Station Kallang.* RNZAF Official PR7110, via Air Force Museum, Christchurch

and taken off back to Palembang on Sumatra. I said, 'Well, we'll try and get a barge or a boat of some kind, and try and sail out of it.'

> *Ian and his mates managed to get aboard the* **Empire Star,** *which was leaving Singapore for Sumatra. As the ship left port it was attacked by Japanese aircraft.*

We saw about eight of what turned out to be Japanese dive-bombers, and they came in and got three

Sharing food on board SS Empire Star *on the voyage from Singapore to Java, February 1942.* Ray Ansdell collection

Right: *On board SS* Empire Star. RNZAF Official HIST612, via Air Force Museum, Christchurch

hits on the boat. The front hold was left open, there were no hatches on it, and it was just full of troops. The nurses were down that hold, and if a bomb had landed in that hold it would have been chaos.

What were the casualties?

I was told there was only about 18. I was on the deck by a mast and I had my revolver with me. As they came in I was firing at them with a revolver, which is pretty pathetic. But then the deck was covered in machine-gun fire, the bullets were bouncing off the deck. There was only a few of us left standing after that one. One bomb landed a few feet away—went right through a cabin, through the deck and into a cabin with eight officers playing cards. That was the end of them. On deck there were corpses lying everywhere, just pulp. There was a chap next to me, he lost his eyesight with the blast and I helped him down the ladder to the galley, told him to stay there and I hopped back up again. I think that probably a few more were blasted over the side.

What did you do with the bodies?

They just pulled them to one side. I suppose somebody looked after them after that. With all the civilians and children looking down from the top deck onto the scene I felt terrible, and I was trying to get these bodies to one side so they couldn't see them.

After that the Japanese came over with formations of 27. At one time we had two lots of 27 from different directions and at different heights. The captain, as soon as the bombers came over, he'd either steer hard right or hard left. This time he just stopped the boat and put the engine astern, and not one bomb hit. The whole boat seemed to jump right out of the water. The next day was 13 February and nothing happened. We got to Java on the 13th—Batavia [now Jakarta].

We slowly got flying again there. I think some planes were already flying, but we didn't fly until a day or two later. Shortly after that they declared Batavia an open city. It meant all the troops had to leave and no fighting could take place.

There weren't many boats leaving, because by that time they'd nearly all been sunk. I didn't worry about getting out. I was still fighting. We were now under the command of Queen Wilhelmina, the Dutch Queen. The remaining squadrons—232, 258, and 148—were all banded together and called 242 Squadron from then on. But declaring Batavia an open city meant we couldn't use the civil 'drome, the military 'drome, and we had to evacuate from there pretty shortly to Bandoeng. We saw the Japanese

landing to the west and the east, just a few miles away. The troops were landing from two lanes of about 12 transport boats, and there were about half a dozen battleships. The barges were coming into the beach with troops in, and we were strafing them coming along the causeway. That was all pretty hectic. We just obeyed orders, did what we were told—'Keep fighting'.

We landed at Bandoeng. We'd only been there a few hours, I suppose, and over came the bombers again, but at a low level this time. I'd just taken off, hardly got off the airfield and my cockpit was full of white glycol fumes. I had no option but to do a sharp bank round and land again, then I had to taxi back to where the planes were kept, and jump out of the plane into a slit trench. By that time I could see about four bombers coming directly at me, then I could see bombs coming straight for me. Bang, bang, bang, bang, and the next one went over my head and landed on a Dutch bomber just a few yards away. The bomber was pointing at me, and as it went on fire it collapsed on the ground and the guns started. They were firing right over my head. Every time I poked my head out these bloody machine guns were firing over my head. I was pretty hopping mad. I found out later that some bloke had left the cap off my glycol tank. That's what caused it. That was about the last operational trip I did, I think.

We retreated further down the country to Tasik Malaya, and by that time we only had about four planes left. I went down by jeep. By that time the Japanese were all over the island. Just a few hours after that they waved the white flag and everybody officially became prisoner of war. We were supposed to stay, report to the different staging spots and hand ourselves over. I was still at the aerodrome when we got the news, on stand-by.

And what was your reaction?
That was it. By that time nearly all the planes—the bombers, the big transport planes, and flying boats— they'd left, and all the ships had either left or been sunk. There was no way off the country.

Java surrendered on 8 March 1942 together with all remaining Allied forces. The surrender appeared to have been based on our demise as an operational unit, that's what I think anyhow. All air force were instructed to assemble on a tea plantation just out of Garoet. While we were getting transported, there was a bit of rifle fire going on somewhere. I don't know if it was the Japanese or some of the local Javanese firing at us.

I jacked it up with my mate Dave Kynman that we'd make an escape to the south coast, try and get a boat or something out; might even get a plane. But he'd sprained his ankle and couldn't do it. When we got to the tea plantation we spent one night there. They were going to hand us over the next day to the Japs just up the road a bit. So I took off by myself. I had a parachute bag, a few tins of rations, and half a blanket and a sheet, and a bit of toilet gear and stuff, and off I went. The tea plantation was in a bit of a basin in the mountains in central Java. I thought, Well I'll climb up that hill there and see where I'm going, and I'll head down towards the south coast along the ridges. Keep away from the roads.

It rained every day just about, and I had a pair of shorts and a shirt. I was wet through half the time and then hot and cold. Getting through the jungle was pretty hard going. I lost my direction a few times. At the end of the first day it rained like hell. In the morning I looked at the sun and found I'd been going in the wrong direction. I looked down and I could see the camp. I hadn't gone very far at all. But I kept on along the ridges. There were what looked like black leopards jumping along the tops of the trees; they had long tails on them. Or monkeys. They kept following me. I fired a few shots at them. On the ground I kept jumping over snakes, grey ones and coloured ones.

Later on I came to a few tracks. A few natives gave me bananas and drinks. The Javanese were okay. I spent that night in the tent, was up at daybreak, a bit of a wash and a bit of tinned food, tinned cheese, and I set off again, steering by the sun. I had a canvas sheet that I'd acquired somewhere off some bed, and it was about two metres by a metre when it was folded double. When it rained I'd climb inside like a tunnel and I was quite dry.

Where did you think you were going?

I was going to go back to either Australia or India. I was going to get down the south coast and just work my way along in a little boat or something, probably disguise myself like a native. The old feet got pretty blistered and I tried to cut a tree down to make a raft at one time. Cut this log and it went straight to the bottom.

Then I came across another rubber plantation, and they took me in there and gave me some sandwiches and coffee. It was absolutely marvellous after a few days out in the open. He said, 'You'd better give yourself up. Wasting your time.' I said, 'Oh no, no.' And off I went again. A few more days out in the open, then I was walking along a road and I came across a little coolie hut, sort of a dosshouse. I hopped in there, and that night I managed to heat up a tin of beans on the fire in the hut. It was marvellous to have a night dry and a bit of warm food. Then I walked with the coolies along the main road, stuck to the road.

SOME CELLS OF BOEI GLODOK PRISON BATAVIA. 320 MEN WERE CONFINED IN THESE THREE CELLS.

Sketch of Boei Glodok Prison, Batavia, by Ian Newlands. 320 men were confined in these three cells.
Ian Newlands collection

After a few more days I came on another plantation and the bloke took me in. He said, 'The hut down there, there's some army chaps.' British. A day or two later the plantation manager had to go to the Japanese for questioning, so we thought, We can't stop here. If they know he's harbouring us he'll be decapitated. So we went back and joined an army convoy and got back up to Garoet school, where I handed myself over to the Japanese.

Ian was taken by train to Batavia and put in captivity there. He became sick with dysentery and dengue fever. In October 1942 he was sent to Japan by sea, via Singapore.

The weather was fairly good on that trip, and we got two meals a day. We survived that trip. We got to Changi [in Singapore] and had about a week or so there. It was an open-air prison. I went on a few working parties, clearing scrub and stuff. I met quite a few of the chaps we'd left behind there. They gave us all the news.

What was the next leg of the journey like?

It wasn't too good. We went up in a convoy of about four or five freighters and four or five destroyers, I'm not sure now. All coal-burning. We used to get down in the coal bunker and keep feeding the coal up towards the furnace so that the stokers could feed the furnace without having to get too far back. That was OK in the fine weather, but later we got into a typhoon. The ship was rolling and pitching, and the coal was sliding down this way and that. You were trying to shovel the coal and stand up and make sure that you didn't get buried in the stuff, and you were black from top to bottom because there was no way of getting washed.

What were your living conditions like on that ship?

The decks were four feet high. One of the boiler pipes burst. We had to go for repairs, so we got out of the convoy and were on our own. A day or two later we got back on the way to Japan again and we struck the typhoon. The toilets got washed away in the storm with people in them. Never saw them again. From then on we were just using rice buckets after we'd eaten the rice. With the boat pitching around they fell down to the bottom. I don't know what happened to the people down at the bottom, because they would have these buckets crashing down on top of them. We were all half stupid, lack of air and food I suppose. Half of them were seasick. I think there might have been a bit of typhoid. It was a real hell trip.

When we got to Japan we were climbing up onto the deck and trying to get down on the wharf in our tropical outfits. The snow was coming down. Some of the Japanese civilians on the wharf saw the funny side of it. They couldn't help laughing. A lot of us still had tropical helmets on. Original khaki shirt and pair of shorts.

I'd say at least a quarter had died on that trip. I got into a truck and ended up in the local hospital at Moji, that's on the southern island of Japan, Kyushu. I was pretty weak. I didn't feel like walking anywhere. We all had bad dysentery. It was a local hospital—a big building with one storey as far as I remember it, concrete floors and rooms opening off a corridor. There were about eight people in each

Ian Newlands' metal food dish, on which he has engraved the places and dates of his incarceration by the Japanese. Alison Parr

room. We were lying on straw palliasses. We had blankets, so that was all right, we were warm enough. The snow was almost up to the windows.

Did they give you any more clothes?

I don't think at that stage we had any more. We had some little things called hand warmers. They were like a spectacle case. They had charcoal burners inside them and you'd get two each. Surprising the amount of warmth that came out of them.

There were no guards there, just a few medical orderlies. We were too weak to walk. The toilets were down the corridor and were typical Japanese style—you squatted. Spent about a third of your time just squatting over the toilet and lying back exhausted on your bed again. The food went straight through, especially the little yellow beans they gave us now and again. They were really oily and they could pass right through your system in about a quarter of an hour. Incredible. You'd hear them hitting the deck like a hailstorm when you went to the toilet. You passed blood and slime. Your weight went down and down very fast. I was down to about half my weight, seven stone. I was about 13 stone in my prime, I suppose. So anyone who wants to lose weight, try a bit of that dysentery stuff. I don't think there was much treatment until we'd been there a month or two.

There were eight of us in this room. We swapped yarns and where we came from, said what we did in our own country. I think they were all air force, ground staff and might have been driving lorries or batmen or something. I know one chap was a gentleman's gentleman. Another one used to look after pigeons.

Were there any deaths while you were there?

More deaths there than anywhere. The next room to us, only one bloke survived. He came and knocked on the door and wanted to know if he could come into us when one of our blokes had been taken out. He had bad beriberi. We all had bad beriberi. You couldn't feel a thing, but we could definitely smell it. We said, 'Have you had an accident in your bed?' He had. The next day it got worse and he said, 'I'll put my hand down and feel', and he put his hand down in the bedclothes and pulled it out covered in faeces. The whole bed was a mess. They took him out, bed and all. We never heard what happened to him. He couldn't feel a thing. About half of them must have died there, I think. When they died they put them in these wooden tubs in a foetal position, and they were cremated. They put their ashes in little wooden boxes about nine inches cubed, with a name on it.

They came along one day and said, 'We're going to give you all this blood plasma.' They had a hell of a job getting these great big blunt needles into our veins. They were American medical orderlies. Fellow prisoners, as far as I know. It took about an hour or so pumping it in, and then, you would never believe it, but we just all got up and walked immediately after getting the blood. You couldn't believe it. The next day they gave us another shot, and said, 'Right, everybody down to the station now. You're going up to north Japan.' First of all we went on a tram down the main road, and then we got on the trains and went through an underground tunnel connecting that island to the mainland. After about a day we ended up in Tokyo and transferred to another train. We had to march up the main street and got booed and spat on by all the young ones.

Before we left that hospital they kitted us out in Japanese army uniforms. Long-john underwear and long trousers; shirts, tunics and greatcoats. We still had our own boots, they didn't have anything in the way of footwear for us. After being in the train a while our feet and legs swelled up and I couldn't get my boots on.

They took us right up to the north of Honshu, the mainland, then we got on a roll-on roll-off ferry across the strait and got over to Hakodate, the southern port of Hokkaido. We got presented with two or three great big hot potatoes, cooked. It was marvellous. Then we were on the train again up to Muroran, which is about another six-hour journey. We arrived at midnight. We stopped right in the middle of nowhere, in the wilderness. Everybody out. Rifle butts up your bum, pushing you out. You stepped down off the carriage onto this great plain of icy snow. We all went flat on our faces, on our backs. Then we had to march about a mile into the camp. Everybody had to strip off in front of the local hospital hut. By that time I'd developed a great big lump under my armpit, blood poisoning, about tennis-ball size.

They said, 'Work tomorrow', and I said, 'No, I'm crook', so they said, 'OK, you can stay home.' We hardly seemed to be asleep for an hour or two, and then everybody had to get up before daylight. We had a bit of rice and soup, lined up outside, then went off to work.

Did you go to work the next day?
No, I didn't.

Ian arrived at Hakodate No. 1 prison camp in Muroran in February 1943. He describes the camp.

Weatherboard walls and wooden shingle roofs, sliding windows and doors. Each hut held about 32 people and a brick path ran from one end of the hut to the other, with a door at either end so all the huts were lined up. You could walk along the path from one end of the camp to the other doing roll calls and things. There were about 15 huts and a separate row for the toilets. The guardhouse was just inside the entrance gate, and they had their own dining room and bathhouse.

There was no barbed wire, just a wooden paling fence. If you wanted to get out of the camp you could just knock a board off and walk out, except they had a few guard dogs, big Alsatians. We couldn't go anywhere because we looked so different to anybody else.

What would have happened if you had escaped, though?
If you tried to escape, they threatened they'd incarcerate the whole hut you escaped from, and if the whole hut escaped, they put the whole camp on detention. If anybody was caught stealing food, they put the whole camp on parade until somebody owned up.

An example of a prisoner of war camp in Japan. This is the main entrance of Fukuoka Camp 17 at Omuta in Kyushu.
Australian War Memorial, Neg. P01662.002

One chap was caught stealing food?

Yes, a Javanese Dutchman. He was made to stand outside the guardhouse in the cold and hold a wooden barrel over his head. Every hour or so he'd put the tub down and they'd give him a good bashing, and then he'd stand up again with the tub over his head. He died eventually. That was probably one of the main cases against the commandant who authorised it. The commandant was hanged shortly after the war as a war criminal.

Beatings were pretty often, mainly just a slap with the open hand, but they'd have a fair swing at you. I got one or two myself here and there. One job was to stoke the Japanese bathhouse furnace. You had to get down early, about nine o'clock in the morning after your breakfast, get the fire going and shovel the coal. I didn't have a clue how all these bloody pipes worked. You checked on the water now and again.

They had their baths. There was a very nice Japanese secretary—she had hers first, and then the commandant would have his, then the lieutenant, the sergeant and then the corporals and so on down. They were all finished, and I looked inside the dining room. There was a tub of rice sitting on the table, a wee bit in the bottom, so I had a handful. I was chewing that and the bloody guard came in. Whack! Whack! Apparently that was their ration, and I was eating it. He didn't say anything to anybody else, he stood me there at attention, and he whacked me and he whacked me and he whacked me and he punched me, tried to knock me out, hitting my jaw. I just stood there. I thought, If he reports me to the commandant I'll be a goner. I had to stand there and take it. He kept punching me until he was exhausted, then he said, 'Forget it.'

When the news was bad—say they'd been losing the war—at two in the morning they'd get you all out of bed. It'd be freezing cold, might be 30 below zero. One night a guard came along and got everybody out of bed and said, 'You will stand in the brick path.' He got up on the beds, about two foot up, so he could be about level with us. He was a smaller bloke. He gave everybody about four hits each, bash, bash, with a fire shovel across the face. It wasn't too bad; didn't seem to kill anybody.

Did your family know where you were?

No, not for about 18 months. It was probably at least a year after I was a prisoner of war, but they wouldn't have known where I was after I left England.

I know it was 18 months at least before they knew I was alive and before we got any letters, or before we could write any notes home. You had a limit of 25 words, I think it was, and that was pretty hard on them, too.

So did you get any mail from them at any stage?

Yes, we did get the odd card. When the war finished we got about three at once. Red Cross, we got one parcel, one full one. We had a few bits and pieces which you might have to parcel up between about eight of you.

Did you stay in the same hut with the same chaps through most of this?

Right through. About 30 or 32 to a hut. We had two huts of British and then there were about 300 Javanese, so there'd be 10 huts. Two years later another party of British soldiers came in, army, about 200 of them. So at one time there must have been close on 600 people in the camp.

Food was scarce.

We got mainly rice and a few potatoes. Actually, if you worked hard you preferred to eat rice than potatoes, because the potatoes gave you indigestion all the time. The soup varied; it was pretty watery sometimes.

We hardly ever talked about sex or told any smutty yarns, just about food. I was brought up in the country. We used to have porridge every morning and eggs and bacon, and Mother used to make all sorts of cakes and we had great roasts of mutton. We got to Canada and had good food and then bang, onto nothing. The chaps that had come from London were used to living on bread and dripping, they hardly noticed the difference. But poor old me, used to all this stuff, I went right down.

You'd think about food all the time. If some bloke had a recipe, you'd write it down. I was going to make them when I got home after the war.

Ian spent three years as a prisoner of war.

The trouble was that if you didn't work you only got about a quarter ration—you got the scum off the top of the rice when they cooked it, which was all rice water, or a little bit of watery soup. On that diet you couldn't improve and you keep getting dysentery and diarrhoea. Somehow or other I got discharged from the hospital. As one way of getting back on my feet again I tried eating grass, making salads, picking bits of clover. In the season I used to get a few runner beans and cook up a few green beans, anything that was going. One day a rabbit appeared suddenly, and somebody left the door open and it ended up under my shirt. It made a nice stew, cooked in the water bottle which hung on the side of the stove. You could make a little tin dixie with a lid on it, it was under the stove in the embers, and if you managed to whip a bit of flour you could make half-pie bread stuff. The water bottles were aluminium. You had a hook on your bottle and could hook it on the side of the stove. It would cook away there, bubble, bubble.

I never got strong enough to go on the parties shovelling iron ore and sand and coal, and lifting the heavy cast-iron ingots and stuff they used to make, so I got inside the workshop. It was a big steelworks, and we were repairing the rolling stock because this particular company owned the whole port. They owned the steamers and the railways, the steel mill and the village. We were repairing railway wagons

Ian Newlands (rear left) after the war had ended but before he was released from Nisi Asibetu camp,
August 1945. Ian Newlands collection

and locomotives, putting bearings in the wheels. We had to straighten them up, put new timber planks on the sides—a big job. You'd have to cut out bent axles underneath and take them to the forge, make them up and weld them.

The guards would take you there in the morning and then you'd be under civilian guards, so you didn't get too much supervision but they'd give you hell now and again. My bloke was pretty good, he was the carpenter, the boss. He was just a skinny little bloke, but he was good as gold. We had a team of about six or seven. There was a Dutchman, he'd done a bit of engineering in Java, and there were Javanese. They were all nice chaps.

> *Towards the end of the war, Ian was shifted to Nisi Asibetu camp, where he and his fellow prisoners*
> *learnt of the end of the war.*

We just had to wait. We were told to stay there. We had survived. Just survived.

He was flown to Yokohama, on to Okinawa and then to Manila in the Philippines. On his return to New Zealand, Ian spent time in Dunedin hospital receiving treatment for his stomach, and was then sent to Hanmer Springs to convalesce. Afterwards he trained as a carpenter in Dunedin and, despite finding it difficult to settle down after his experiences, worked for the Housing Corporation and the Civil Aviation Department. He currently lives in Auckland.

Ian Newlands (rear left) with Australian army officers, also former POWs, on board HMS Formidable. *They are wearing American kit.* Ian Newlands collection

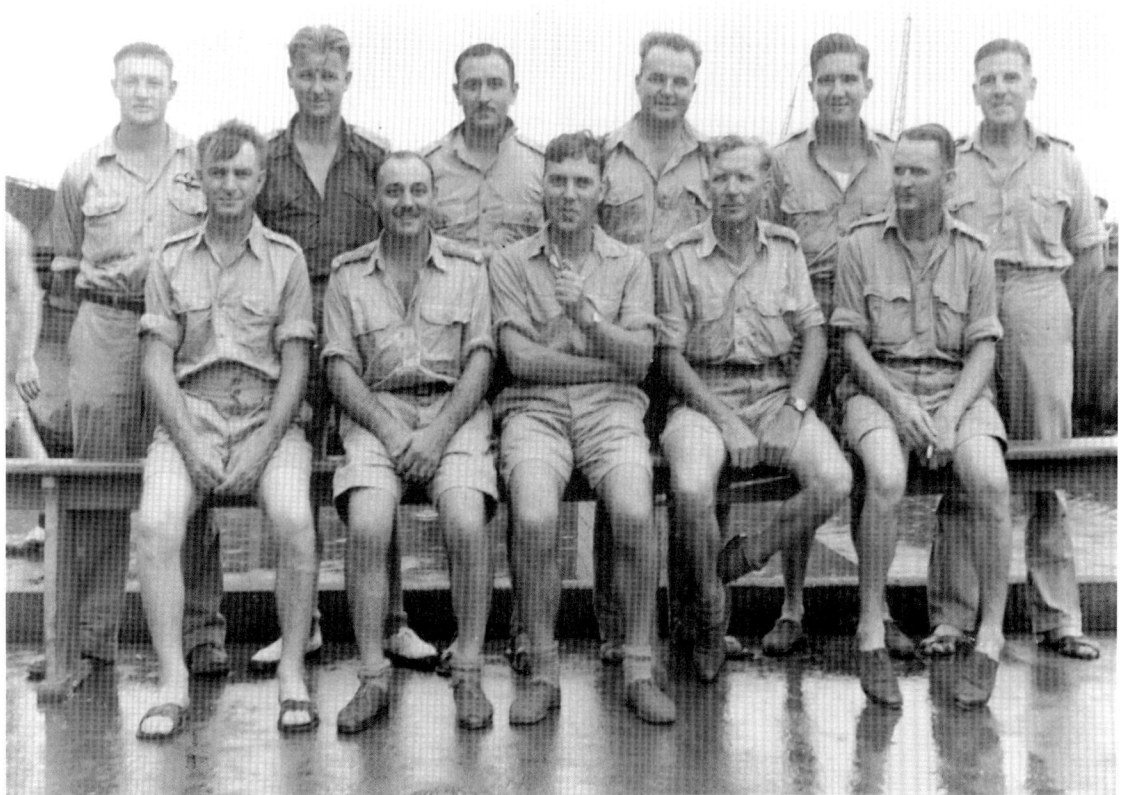

'SINGAPORE ON FIRE'

WILLIAM MITCHELL, 391789, CORPORAL, ROYAL NEW ZEALAND AIR FORCE

Bill Mitchell was born in Dunedin in July 1916. He attended High Street School and Dunedin Technical College before working at temporary jobs during the Depression. Bill was doing his panelbeating apprenticeship when he joined up in 1939. He explains why he enlisted so quickly.

I THINK WE THOUGHT it was a great adventure, and also we were very patriotic. England was the mother country. In the early stages of the war, the air force had training schools at all the railway workshops—Hillside, Addington, Hutt, and Auckland. They had premises at the railway workshops and training officers. We were on what they called the second war course, or flight riggers. At Hillside they had flight riggers' courses and flight mechanics' courses. A flight rigger is somebody who looks after the main fuselage and body and all the systems of the aeroplane. Not the engine, not the radio, and not the electrical parts. The fuselage, which is the body of the aircraft, the brake system, the hydraulic system, the controls, the undercarriage, you name it.

After we finished our flight riggers' course, which was three months, we had exams and some of us were sent to Hobsonville to do a further course and become what they called Fitter 2 As (fitter two [2nd-class] airframes). And a Fitter 2 was supposed to be able to do a complete overhaul on an aeroplane. It was an advanced course, and we had exams to pass out from that.

Previous page: *RNZAF personnel bound for overseas service.* RNZAF Official PR1922, via Air Force Museum, Christchurch
Above: *Bill Mitchell.* William Mitchell collection

In July 1941, Bill and others in an RNZAF party were sent to Singapore in a unit of ground staff attached to the RAF. They were posted to the airbase at Seletar.

What were your initial impressions of Singapore?

The heat, the muggy heat. The luxurious lifestyle of the Europeans, and the poverty and dirt and degradation of the native population. It was filthy. You could smell the Singapore River about a quarter of a mile away. Everything went into the river. It was the colour of mushroom soup. Nowadays it's clean, but in those days it was filthy.

Bill Mitchell (third from right) outside Tiger Balm mansion, Singapore. William Mitchell collection

Did you have a sense there that people knew there was a war coming?

No. They said there won't be any war. The Japanese are far too busy in China and the other areas. They won't come here.

We were based at Seletar, on the north shore of Singapore Island on the edge of the Johor Strait,

Unknown airman holding fruit in front of a Chinese store, Singapore, late 1941. RNZAF Official HIST627, via Air Force Museum, Christchurch

not very far from the naval base. Seletar was enormous. Our first impression was that it was like a huge English park. There was a wrought-iron fence right around the perimeter, and inside everything was landscaped. There were lovely concrete highways and the barracks were painted white with red roofs. It was all very immaculate. There was lots of native labour cutting the grass and doing the gardening. When you first went in you couldn't see any evidence that it was an air force base, but when you got further in and went down the hill you could see the airfield and the hangars down by the shore.

We were quartered in what had been the old school on the base. It was brick—tiled floor, tiled roof, lots of windows with no glass in them, shutters. Big fans in the ceilings, and quite suitable for the temperatures. We had to sleep under mosquito nets, but as I recall we never had any anti-malarial medication because they kept the mosquitoes under control, whereas up in the jungle areas you had to have quinine.

You had a houseboy?

Yes. He was a Tamil. We all put in a few cents and he cleaned our shoes and polished our buttons and kept the place tidy. We called him Tony. I don't know what his name was. He was a handsome fellow, had a moustache and was always dressed in white robes. He would be about 25.

We used to drink enormous amounts of fluid. Somewhere I've still got my old pint mug. We'd have two of those with a meal. Tea. You were sweating all the time. If you had a shower and put on a clean shirt, it would be wet within moments with sweat. It was very uncomfortable.

Sikh houseboy at Kallang airbase, Singapore.
Ray Ansdell collection

What was your job there?

We were there to help them restore four old Singapore flying boats which the RAF had given to New Zealand. At the time New Zealand wanted Catalina flying boats to be based at Fiji to do maritime reconnaissance. We had an area round Fiji that had to be patrolled. At that stage Japan was not in the war, but we still had this area to patrol. Catalinas were in great demand so we didn't get any for quite a while. The RAF said we've got these old Singapores here, we don't know what to do with them. There were Short Singapore Mark IIIs. They were the last big biplane flying boats that the RAF had. We worked with the RAF chaps to restore them. They had to be taken to pieces and repaired and assembled.

Servicing a Singapore Mark III flying boat.
William Mitchell collection

To what extent did you see the RAF station as being on a war footing?

It was amazing. It was almost like a peacetime station. We knocked off at four o'clock in the afternoon; we didn't work at the weekends. There was no urgency about anything. There were very few air-raid shelters because they said that the water table was so high that they would flood. We'd been told that there were bomb-proof concrete hangars there. Well, we never ever found them—because they weren't there. They said there wasn't going to be a war. The rubber planters in Malaya were quite happy to carry on as they were, because they were getting record prices for their rubber. They didn't want a war.

The Japanese attacked without warning.

They bombed Singapore, the Philippines, and Pearl Harbor at the same time. We were asleep, and the next thing there was an almighty explosion and we were more or less blown out of bed. We stumbled out of the barracks and fell into the concrete gutter that was outside, because we didn't know where the air-raid shelter was. Actually, we thought it was the end of the world. It was a rude awakening.

The raid did quite a bit of damage but didn't kill many people. Then they carried on over Singapore city. The lights were on because they couldn't find the bloke who was supposed to turn them off. So the Japanese had the luxury of bombing an illuminated city. It caused quite a few deaths, mainly amongst the Chinese.

Sid Wells manning the ground defences for 488 Squadron at Kallang, Singapore, December 1941. RNZAF Official HIST616, via Air Force Museum, Christchurch

What was the pattern of air raids after that?

Nightly. The Japanese would choose a target and they would pattern-bomb it. They soon found they had control of the air, so they decided it would be better to bomb in the daylight. They used to come over usually every morning and we had to be ready to hop into a shelter.

After that first attack, did the attitude on the station change?

Yes. It became more urgent. All we had on the station at Seletar was a squadron of old Vildebeestes, old biplanes, and they were sent down on several raids. Very few of them came back.

Did it change how you felt about being out of New Zealand?

Yes, it did. It felt sort of hopeless, in that we were constantly on the back foot because of our inferior aircraft and the superiority of the Japanese. They were unstoppable at that stage.

They made us into what they called the 'Fly In' Repair Group, and we worked at night to escape the bombing. We repaired aircraft that had been damaged but were still able to fly. They flew them into us and we repaired them and they took them away again. Things were getting worse and worse, there were fewer and fewer aircraft to work on and the bombing was getting even more frequent. They were starting to pick a particular target each day and give it a real pasting, and a lot of the bombings were being done on the docks in Singapore. We didn't know what was going to happen to us because we had no officers and we had no clout.

Evidently, if you were a technical person or aircraft maintenance person you were deemed worthy of evacuating. And somehow, somewhere, somebody decided that we were to be evacuated, but we couldn't find our sergeants to sign the forms. 'Stony' Homer, one of our corporals, said, 'I'll fix this.' If it hadn't been for him we might not have got out.

We had been down to the docks the night before and had worked all night loading equipment into the ships—it was subsequently lost in the Japanese bombing. Singapore looked a real mess at that stage. There were fires burning and wrecked buildings and it looked like a doomed city. We didn't believe the newspapers, because they were censored. They kept saying that the Japanese were being held, but we knew that they were miles further south than was reported. The military would never admit that they were being defeated.

The effect of a Japanese air raid on Kallang airbase, Singapore. Ray Ansdell collection

We were very scared. We didn't know what was going to happen to us. We were looking around for a boat. A lot of people stole launches and went to Sumatra, and they were picked up later by the Japanese.

Did you think the air force had forgotten you?

Yes. We never had any communication from anybody after we were left there. When the squadron leader went on the last flying boats he said, 'I'll see that you men are evacuated.' We never saw him again for 40 years.

How did you get away in the end?

We were told to be down at the docks at dusk. This was 31 January. Singapore fell on 15 February. The Japanese were starting to bombard Singapore Island as we left, from over the other side of the straits with their artillery, that's how close they were. A few days after that, they landed on Singapore Island.

We were told to be down at the docks to embark on a ship. We made sure we were there with the papers signed. We got to the docks, and there had been an air raid. A lot of the warehouses were on fire. There was smoke everywhere, and on the wharf was a great pile of cartons and boxes and assorted packages, and they said, 'All this has got to be loaded onto the ship before we can go.' There was a crowd of English servicemen standing there, doing nothing, and we said, 'By gosh, this is no good', so we started heaving all this stuff onto the ship. We had to put it on the deck because there was no room underneath. We piled it wherever we could. And when that was all loaded, we sailed. It was just at dusk.

Everything looked as if it was falling apart in Singapore, great clouds of smoke and fires after the bombing. Two large American troopships had just sailed to get out of it, the *Manhattan* and the *West Point*. We got outside the harbour into a minefield. The skipper said, 'I can't see the marks, we can't move. We'll have to anchor here overnight until we can see the marks in the morning.' We thought, This is great, good start. Moored in a minefield with Singapore on fire.

We were on HMS *Kedah*. It was crowded with refugees. There were women and children, service personnel, and various other people who were escaping. The women and children were accommodated below in cabins as much as possible, but there were no cabins left to us so we remained on deck in amongst all the cartons and packages. When we wanted to have a meal we just opened the nearest carton. If there was tin in it, we opened the tin and ate whatever was in the tin. It was quite an interesting menu. We never had knives or forks, so if anybody had a pocket knife that was valuable. One morning we all had a shave courtesy of Bill Wellington, who lent us his razor and a mug full of suds, but otherwise things were just as they were. We slept on deck wherever we could find a place to have forty winks when not on watch. But it was an amazing experience to be on that boat with all those people and get away from Singapore.

In the morning we started off again and had to keep a lookout for Japanese aircraft. We were lucky, we never saw any, and that night we were passing through the Bangka Strait. We were on bridge watch because they'd found that our eyesight was better in the dark than the Malayan seamen. There were several ships around. We didn't know whether they were friend or foe, and you couldn't do much about it. We got through the Bangka Strait without being bombed and the next day we arrived at Batavia. We disembarked there. We went to a Dutch barracks called Laan Trevaali and stayed there for several days, not knowing what was going to happen.

RNZAF personnel climb aboard a supply ship, May 1945. RNZAF Official PR6732, via Air Force Museum, Christchurch

How many days were you on that boat?
Three days.

> *From Batavia they travelled by ship to Sumatra, then back to southern Java, where they joined a convoy en route to Australia. In Adelaide they joined the ship* **Durban Castle** *and returned to New Zealand. Bill was ordered to Gisborne, where he met and married Joy Brooking in December 1943. In February 1944 he was posted to the Pacific.*

I never volunteered to go over to the islands, I was just ordered to go.

We were told that we were going overseas some time or other when we were re-equipped with new aircraft, Grumman Avengers.

They arrived in Espiritu Santo in the New Hebrides, and then travelled by ship to Empress Augusta Bay in Bougainville.

We had to crawl down the cargo nets on the side of the ship with our backpacks and our rifle, and into a 'duck'. These were amphibious trucks, very versatile. There would be about 30 or 40 of us in the duck and they transported us from the ship to the beach. When it got to the beach they just drove out, disconnected the propeller and engaged the wheels. And drove us to our camp, which was inland.

It was a beautiful big bay with surf all round it, a lovely place to swim. It was dangerous actually, but it was a lovely beach. We didn't see much on the truck going to the camp. It was jungle.

The Americans didn't conquer the whole of Bougainville, they just secured a beachhead—a semi-circular area with a defended perimeter and two or three airfields within that. That's all they wanted. It was a place from where they could bomb Rabaul. A forward base. There were still a lot of Japanese on the island, over on the other side.

We knew they were there, but we felt safe because of the defended perimeter. We had the odd air raid, not from Bougainville but from further north. The Japanese were still very strong around the other coast and down the south, as we found out when they decided that they'd recapture the airfields. The Japanese launched a major offensive and assembled up above us in the jungle. The Americans knew about it because of the Fijian commandos. They'd got out in amongst them and found out what the Japs were up to. The Americans laid down an artillery barrage where the Japanese were congregating and killed thousands of them. There were supposed to be 13,000 killed there.

Did you hear that happening?

Yes. It was night-time. The shells were going over us. They had cruisers in the bay; they were firing too. All around us there were these 155-millimetre howitzers, and every time one of them fired our tent would shake. We guessed by the explosions getting closer that the Japanese were advancing.

Number 2 Servicing Unit performs maintenance on a Chance Vought Corsair at Piva airstrip, Bougainville. RNZAF Official PR4629, via Air Force Museum, Christchurch

Were you scared?

Yes. We had an air-raid shelter in our tent. Our tent was down below the ground, they'd dug it down and sandbagged it round and they'd built an air-raid shelter off the side of the tent. The first time we dived into it when there was an air raid, we dived out quicker, because there was a snake in it.

Bill's camp was located at Piva airstrip, near the defended perimeter of the American enclave.

There were two airstrips, and just up the road was where all the action was taking place. It would be about a kilometre away. You could hear everything. There was a lot of automatic rifle fire and artillery

shells. They'd cleared the jungle at the perimeter so they had a clear area of fire. The Yanks had dug themselves in, in pillboxes.

We were supposed to be the third line of defence. They had the perimeter and they had a second line and a third line. We were supposed to get in little shallow foxholes which looked remarkably like graves, and fire our rifles at the Japanese. We had American Springfield rifles. You had to put a plug in the barrel to keep the mason bees out. They used to build their nests in the barrels. It was like concrete and if you fired one the barrel would burst, so everybody had to plug up the barrel of the rifle. You had to know all these little tricks.

We were told to be ready, but we were never called. The Japanese did break through in various places, but they never got past the second line.

When you went up to what had been the front line the next day, what did you see?
It was unbelievable. For a start there were no trees. It was dense jungle, and all that was left were a few shattered stumps. The rest of it was like a ploughed field from all the shell bursts. There was equipment everywhere, spent cartridges, rifles. Debris everywhere. It was frightening. The smell of death. The Americans had bulldozed great big holes and pushed all the corpses in and put in quicklime in the front line, but up in the hills you couldn't do that and there were arms and legs and limbs sticking out everywhere. The smell. Dead bodies.

When we came back from that front line we couldn't eat our lunch. The smell of dead bodies in the tropics is something else. It's something you can't get rid of. It was upsetting.

We made friends with some of the American soldiers. They used to come and see us. They were good. They were living like rats in a hole underground. They had automatic weapons and pillboxes and round the pillboxes they had nets, like fishing nets, because the Japs used to crawl up and try and throw a grenade into the pillbox. The Japanese grenades weren't very good, not like ours. Some of them used to crawl through the barbed wire and entanglements and the minefield and come and watch the pictures. The Yanks had movies up at the front line.

There were Japanese snipers in the trees around us when we arrived at that camp. The Japs used to tie themselves up in the tree with a rifle and do all their sniping. There were a few bullets whizzing around the camp when we arrived. We were told to be careful.

Our aircraft didn't arrive till that artillery barrage was over. The Japs had guns up in the mountains

Corsair taking off from Piva airstrip. RNZAF Official PR4622, via Air Force Museum, Christchurch

there. The aircraft took off from Torokina over to the hills, dropped their bombs on the Jap artillery—which they couldn't find because they were in a cave—then came back again.

After time on Bougainville, Bill was sent back to Guadalcanal.

I must tell you about a trip we did on Guadalcanal. We had a day off and we wanted to go from Guadalcanal to Cape Esperance, which is on the northwest tip. We had a jeep and a great big Chevrolet 4 x 4 truck, and we had what they call a cherry picker. This was a smaller truck with a crane on it. First-off the roads were reasonably good, and then we got into the jungle and the road deteriorated. It got worse and worse. We were going through creeks, and the only vehicle that didn't get stuck was our big 4 x 4 truck, because it had great big wheels and four-wheel drive and an old Chevy engine, very strong. All the others got stuck and had to pull themselves out. At the start we had a canopy and the whole lot got wiped off in the jungle. We finally got to Cape Esperance and there was a Catholic mission station

there, completely ruined. It had been shelled. The Japs had had a strongpoint there. But all the way along the north shore of Guadalcanal it was like a military museum. There were Japanese ships that had been beached. There was even a midget submarine with its conning tower open and there were barges and landing craft, derelict, lying all along that beach. It was amazing.

The parcels we got from home were wonderful. Quite often we'd go back to the tent and make a cup of tea and have some good old New Zealand fruitcake. They used to pack them in a round biscuit

Left: *Patriotic parcels for the troops are unloaded in the Pacific.* ATL, War History Collection, F-41657-1/2
Above: *Performing maintenance on a Corsair, Piva, 1944.* RNZAF Official PR4616, via Air Force Museum, Christchurch

tin and cover it with canvas, and no matter what you did to that tin, the old cake would survive and we would eventually get it. It was amazing. Quite often that was our lunch. We also got parcels from the patriotic fund. At one stage we couldn't understand why we never got any parcels. It was because our equipment officer was intercepting them and selling them.

> *Bill was on Guadalcanal for around six weeks while the Corsair aircraft arrived, and then went to the Green Islands, where he spent about six months as groundcrew. The conditions in which they serviced the aircraft were quite primitive.*

We worked out of tents, and I went onto the flights. That meant you had to get up early in the morning, get four or five Corsairs away to patrol off Rabaul, be there when they came back, service them, refuel them, do anything that was required. You had a free period in the middle of the day, then you had to go back later on and do another lot. I found that quite a change after being in the workshops, where you worked from eight to five every day. You felt you were more involved in the actual operations.

We lost six or eight Corsairs one day in a tropical storm. It was terrible. They had to bail out or ditch, and they all got lost. That was between Rabaul and Green Island. The weather reports were misleading, and they got caught in a storm and couldn't find the island. Ran out of fuel, most of them. It was a major disaster because it was preventable up to a point, if the weather report had been accurate.

Did they seem to have any sense of apprehension when they were flying?
No, the madder you were, the better fighter pilot you were. You had to be a bit of a tearaway, and a good shot. The old sober types, they put them on the bombers.

Did you have any contact at all with the local people?
Not very much on Green, but on Bougainville and Guadalcanal it was amazing. They would come into your tent and they'd have all sorts of souvenirs for sale that they'd pinched. A bloke would come in with a row of wristwatches right up his arm—probably stolen from corpses—and various souvenirs like fountain pens and rings, and try and flog these off. Americans were great on trying to hock off Japanese skulls, and those curved swords. They were vastly prized. Skulls that they found. There were bones all over the place. I wouldn't have anything to do with it. Macabre.

Bill returned to New Zealand in early 1945, having spent six years in the air force.

When I got back to New Zealand and went to Ohakea I was quite downhearted because I missed my old friends. My health had suffered and I had what I would call a minor breakdown. I couldn't become interested in the job. They sent me to Rotorua, to Brent's Hotel. That was supposed to be a place where you recuperated.

Do you feel you should have been brought home sooner?

It would have been better for my health, but I can understand their reasons. If you kept changing everybody it upset the whole working of the outfit. You had to wait for a replacement. They brought so many replacements up every week. And until your replacement arrived, you had to stay.

It was a marvellous experience, and it took you to places that you'd never go. It made you realise how lucky you were—getting out of Singapore, and getting through those experiences in the islands, because there were plenty who didn't. You could get on a plane and never be seen again, and that happened to plenty.

I don't feel resentment to the Japanese. I've had two or three Japanese cars and they've been good. Some people won't buy a Japanese car on principle. I hold a grudge against the military hierarchy because of the mess they made of Singapore.

On board SS Empire Star *as it neared Batavia.*
Ray Ansdell collection

Being married was the main thing, and having a wife you could respect and love, that was the thing that carried you through. Bringing up a family, that kept you amused.

Bill and Joy have four daughters. After the war he continued working in panelbeating, eventually owning his own business in Oamaru.

'THE PACIFIC ISLANDS
WERE IN DANGER'

HARRY BIOLETTI, 64323,
LIEUTENANT, 29 AND 30 BATTALIONS

Harry Bioletti was born in Auckland in 1913. He was a military cadet at Takapuna Grammar School, and then a cadet for the Auckland Star *newspaper before travelling to Australia and England. He has some memories of the First World War, which ended when he was five years old.*

I CAN JUST REMEMBER soldiers of the First World War in their puttees, wound round their legs. I remember Armistice Day because down in Takapuna all the flags were on the shops. I can't remember any bands, but the whole place was decorated.

Can you remember the outbreak of war?

Yes, certainly. In 1938 businesses started digging holes in the concrete for their employees to get into in case the Germans came over. I was in Birmingham. I travelled on the Continent in 1938 and watched the rise of Hitlerism. When I was in Innsbruck I watched the midnight parades of the SS, carrying their Nazi flags and singing 'Deutschland über Alles' and 'Horst Wessel'. And in Berlin I saw all the wallahs going to their offices in uniform, and as they passed each other, they'd go like this [salute], 'Heil Hitler'. Unbelievable.

Anyway, I was in Birmingham and I can remember sitting on the stairs and listening to Neville Chamberlain—this was 11 o'clock in the morning on a Sunday—saying, 'And consequently, this country is now at war with Germany.' I could see that there was only one thing for me to do—pack up and come home. If I hadn't have done that immediately, I wouldn't have been able to come back, because I wouldn't have got a passage.

Previous page: *Drinking beer in the garden of the convent where Harry Bioletti was stationed in Fiji.* Harry Bioletti collection
Above: *Harry Bioletti.* Harry Bioletti collection

Interior of a hut in Fiji. Note the mosquito netting.
Harry Bioletti collection

In July 1940 Harry joined the Territorials and went into camp at Waiouru. In April 1941 he arrived in Fiji with 29 Battalion.

There were already soldiers there, and we replaced them. They came back and went to the Middle East, and we thought that this was what would happen to us too, possibly.

We stepped ashore, and the first word we learned was 'Bula', which is 'Hello' in Fijian. From there we went over to Namaka, near Lautoka, and were in camp there—the whole battalion. We lived in two-man tents. We didn't have any mattresses, so we used *Auckland Weekly News* to soften the slats. We had mosquito nets—it was imperative to have mosquito nets. You'd wake up in the morning and the mosquitoes had somehow got in, because the nets were full of holes which you'd tied with string, but sometimes they'd get in and they'd be blown up with blood, then you'd squash them.

We were there for a purpose, because Japan was seen as coming into the war, and the Pacific Islands were in danger if Japan was going to move south. Well, where else could it go? It wasn't going to go north against Russia. The only places where the Japs could arrive would be at Lautoka, where they could come through the reef, and so the artillery there up in the heights trained their guns with this in mind. It was our job as the infantry to stop them landing. We dug weapon pits. There's a piece of poetry—hardly poetry; verse, doggerel—that goes:

Oh that army in Fiji

They're as brave as brave can be

And they dug their weapon pits down by the sea.

But as fast as they could build them

The sea came in and filled them

Much to the major's misery.

We would never have been able to contain the Japs, I feel, if they'd landed in numbers. First of all, we still had Lewis machine guns from the First World War. We were unprepared for war and we were unprepared for a tropical war.

Were you getting any news at all about what was going on?
Only through the radio, that I can remember. The BBC. In Namaka our colonel used to give us a rundown on the war. I can remember him telling us—this was at the time of Crete—he said, 'This will tell whether air power is going to beat land power.' In other words, the parachuters were coming down. It was all so far away.

I was interviewed to go for a commission and then we went on a jungle training exercise, then we got a message to report back to camp and were told that we were going to New Zealand to OCTU.

After training at the OCTU in Trentham, Harry was commissioned in June 1942. He was then posted to 30 Battalion as a second lieutenant and went with 3 Division from New Zealand to New Caledonia in October 1942.

I went over there as the advance party and stayed in American camps, ate with the Americans, got to know them. Our job was to find campsites for the different battalions.

We bludged left, right, and centre from them. I don't know that we borrowed—we pinched mostly. One of our jobs was unloading the ships in Noumea. That was for six weeks. Whatever was on the ship, if we wanted one, we pinched one. Like a jungle hammock. Everybody in our battalion had a jungle hammock. We pinched typewriters, if we wanted a typewriter. Down the bottom of the hold would

American 'chow' line, Koumac, New Caledonia. Harry Bioletti collection

be literally hundreds of tins of stuff without anything on the outside to say what was in them because the packets had broken open. They had to do something with all this, so they'd be loaded onto trucks. This was the Americans. But the trucks had New Zealand drivers on them, and they would stop at our camps and unload a lot of this stuff to the boys. They'd have all these tins under their bed and they'd get a bayonet, shove it in, and say, 'Oh shit.' They'd got beetroot.

When you saw African Americans, how were they treated?

We would go to cinemas in New Caledonia, every night in Noumea, big open-air cinemas, and there'd be a fracas somewhere and you knew, sure as hell, it was because a black had started to sit in amongst somebody from Texas or somewhere like that. They weren't combat soldiers for starters, but they were later on.

We went down to Bourail, where there was a divisional sports meeting. There were swimming races, running races, football, there was rugby. There was horse racing at Bourail, and I think some of the soldiers were jockeys. In Noumea we went to the Americans' café, the officers' quarters. Mostly we had to be down on the water, superintending the unloading of the ships.

In August 1943, 30 Battalion left New Caledonia in a convoy of ships bound for Guadalcanal in the Solomon Islands. They stopped in Vanuatu on the way.

We landed in one of the islands of New Hebrides and did a practice landing. We went down the nets, took the stuff ashore, brought it back in, then came up the nets again.

What was it like going down the nets with your full kit on?

It wasn't too good, because your rifle was inclined to swing out. You had to hang on, so you always put your hand on the vertical ropes and not the horizontal ropes, because the man above would put his feet on your hands if you weren't careful. Some soldiers froze on the nets, couldn't go up and couldn't go down. When you got to the bottom, you had to wait for the rise of the waiting boat. When it came up, you jumped in. You didn't jump when it was going down, and you didn't jump between the waiting boat and the side of the ship.

The coxswain couldn't always keep the boat hard up against the hull of the ship, sometimes there was a gap there. You'd look over your shoulder or the coxswain or somebody who was in the boat would say, 'Jump!' But there were quite a number of men horizontally going down at the same time, you were not the only one. People fell in the sea, too. They were carrying a lot of weight with their gear and their rifle on.

Harry recalls that Guadalcanal was a staging post and they did not encounter many Japanese until they moved forward through the Solomon Islands.

There may have been a stray Jap back in the jungle—a loner—but apart from that, no. I can remember one night, I think we were playing a bit of bridge, and I kept going sniff, sniff. Anyhow, next morning I ratted around outside and there was a dead Jap buried outside the tent.

One night Washing Machine Charlie came over—he was a Japanese lone pilot—and all hell broke loose around him. He used to come over every night, apparently, from not too far up north. Everybody knew it because the Japanese engine was not synchronised like the American one. There was a sort of a gap and you could pick it. It sounded like a washing machine. We saw him shot down. You could see the tracer bullets aiming at this thing and then it disappeared in flames.

The comfort of a cigarette. ATL, War History Collection, F–41645–1/2

Did you have any contact with Solomon Islanders?

Only when they moved through the camp, and some of them occasionally moved through bare-breasted.
The boys were there with their eyes popping out. That didn't happen very often.

In September 1943 Harry moved to Vella Lavella with 30 Battalion.

We landed near the airfield and then pushed into the hinterland. We were camped on a river's edge and had to have a little ferry, with a rope and some sort of a punt, in order to get across the river. Our job there was to go out and patrol each day, because there were stray Japs around. You never knew what was behind the bush there.

We patrolled up along the coast, in amongst the pandanus trees. I remember a doctor came with us one time. He was going up into a village to act as midwife to a child which was a breech presentation of some sort. We were bombed there. I remember getting into a slit trench because I could hear them coming over, and this mate of mine wouldn't bother. They got closer and closer and dropped a bomb, and he jumped in on top of me and nearly knocked me out.

People were coming and going all the time. Men were being boarded out—by that I mean a medical board—because of sickness. Psychosis in some cases, but mostly it was skin problems—dermatitis.

Japanese prisoners of war, Guadalcanal, c. 1943. Alan Roberts collection

When we first landed there we weren't allowed to have lights at night. The men couldn't play cards, couldn't do anything. The noise in the jungle is just terrific. All these different insects making noises. Then the rains came, and when they came they didn't stop. Incessant. It sort of gets into your brain after a while. And the muck! The great big American trucks were rutted down, and they had to have men to try and get them out of it and the whole of the traffic was held up. But it was the relentless, remorseless rain which got to you. And then the sun came out, and it was OK. But not being able to do anything at night—some of the men would have been carried off for psychiatric treatment if it had carried on too long.

I remember there were Japanese prisoners on Vella Lavella. Where they had come from I'm not sure, but they were all naked except for a handkerchief over the genital area, held with a string. They all had a tin of Chelsea cigarettes in their hand, and were smoking away. The Americans had given them cigarettes. They were being loaded on a ship to be taken, I don't know where, probably to New Zealand. Might have been going to Featherston Camp for all I know. It was absolutely amazing. A couple of hundred Japanese prisoners, nothing on, tin of Chelsea cigarettes, smoking away in most cases, and all these American soldiers with revolvers pointing to the sky as they loaded them onto this ship.

Was that the first time you'd seen Japanese people close up?
Yes, it was. They were very fit looking men, well set-up young people.

The one fear in the jungle was being captured by the Japanese, because they would butcher you physically. The prisoner of war convention meant nothing to them. They didn't subscribe to it.

You could smell Japs. I think it was some sort of talcum powder they used. They were very clean people. You could smell where they'd been. I used to tell the boys, 'No smoking on the trail.' The tobacco smoke would linger around and tell them you'd been there. You could only go through the jungle in one straight line, there was no other way. We were trained not to get into bunches.

In October the battalion moved to Gizo Island, near Vella Lavella.

Gizo was the administrative island for the Solomons, apparently. We weren't sure whether the Japs were there or not. We landed there, charged ashore, and charged into their administration block. They'd all gone. We saw where their revetments or reinforced trenches were. Not only that, but they'd burrowed into the ground, tunnelled their defensive positions there. So if they'd been there, we'd have copped the lot, I rather feel. We did capture one poor hapless Jap who was left behind.

After an overnight stay on Gizo, Harry returned to Vella Lavella. In January 1944 he landed on Nissan Island.

Rest time in the jungle, Nissan Island. Harry Bioletti collection

Your first landing there was a commando raid. What was the purpose of that?

The purpose of it was to enquire how many Japs were there, because the Americans wanted to put an airfield there, right up the top. They had one on Bougainville, which was close by, but they wanted one on Nissan. Or maybe there was one there still and the Japs were using it, and they couldn't afford to have airfields where Japs could take off and bomb shipping, particularly theirs. So it was our job to go up there, find out how many Japs were there and note the condition of the airfield. It was really a reconnaissance to see what was going on up there.

How much were you told about what you were doing?

I saw maps of it. I was a first lieutenant with a platoon. We were on an LCP, landing craft personnel, which takes about 32 men. The landing boats were put over the side and we would get into them on signal, go down the nets on the side of the boat into the LCP. This was all in the dark at night. In my particular boat was the American commander, and I can remember the coxswain of the boat being hesitant, and the commander saying, 'Go in! I order you to go in', because he was hesitant. He had to find his way through the reef, which was pretty damn narrow, I may say. The opening's not very wide and I don't know how the hell he found his way in there, because it sure as hell wasn't moonlight.

Some of the boys were sick. I told them, 'If you're going to be sick, for Christ's sake take your helmet off and be sick into your helmet. Don't spew down the neck of the man in front of you.' Some of the Americans were waiting in their boats for hours, waiting to be called in to reinforce them, and of course they were as sick as hell.

We went in through the opening and turned right, and then turned right again and we landed in the sand. The front went down and we went off the boat, in the dark. We had entrenching tools for digging. You could hear the sand in the night—I don't know how to describe the sound—probably like running your hand over silk. The sound of sand on a shovel. We dug just enough to get down below the top. Then daylight came. We found we were in amongst the coconut palms and there were the natives in front of us. They knew all about it, of course.

They took aerial photos of Green Island—Green, Nissan, I think we called it Green. Aerial photos were taken and around the coast were these structures—they couldn't understand what they were. They looked like buildings of some sort, or enclosures probably. The intelligence people thought they might

Landing day on Nissan Island, 1944, with locals. Harry Bioletti collection

have been Japanese defence positions of some sort. Anyhow, we did land and we found out that these so-called Japanese defensive positions were part of the cargo cult of the Pacific, where they built these things because in the night some ethereal being was going to come and leave all these goods for them. I think it is still extant in the islands, in some parts, even today. That's what these shapes were—stone enclosures.

According to the aerial reconnaissance the island looked fairly clear, as far as we could gather. We did have New Zealand pilots flying over, also on reconnaissance. They were aware that the Japs were there because they had boats inside the lagoon.

We got into the landing craft again and moved down the coast inside the horseshoe. We poked our nose in there. And I heard, and the others heard, the closing of a bolt of a rifle which wasn't ours. Obviously a Jap was in there. We backed off, because we were told not to get into conflict. That wasn't the idea, it was reconnaissance.

But some time later another boat, a landing craft personnel boat, went into this same spot or nearby and walked into a trap with the Japs, and Lieutenant Middleton was killed there and one or two others were wounded.

We weren't there to warn them, we'd gone further on.

In the meantime, people had gone over to the other end of the horseshoe, which is where the airfield was. Their job was to explore the situation for the airfield there. A New Zealand plane flew over and threw a toilet roll, and only afterwards he told us that on the toilet roll was a message to say there was a number of Japs in a certain place on the island. He tried to tell us.

We were there all that day and then we got into our boats to come off again. The tide was going out. We had to keep on getting out of the boats and pushing them out to stay in the water, otherwise we'd have been left on the hard.

We were working strictly to a time schedule. We had to stay in the boat for several hours because we weren't going to meet our rendezvous till midnight. So we kept on pushing the boat out, and staying in the boat, and then we got the signal to move out. We went through the opening and then we saw this one single red light, just a flick, for a few seconds. Then we could hear the voices of the men climbing up the nets and getting back into the destroyer. You couldn't show any more lights than that. It was just intermittent. It was a relief to know that we'd made a rendezvous, otherwise we might have had to go back.

Dense jungle on Nissan Island made visibility poor. Harry Bioletti collection

In February 1944 Harry returned to Nissan.

The whole battalion was going and we were landing in daytime too. The platoon in front of me ran into the Japanese. Could have been me. They were wiped out. We moved further on. The artillery bombed further ahead of us and there was nothing there. I passed a camp where the Japs had been. There was a pair of binoculars hanging on a branch and one of my men pointed and said, 'Look', so I went over and got the binoculars. All their gear was there. We were right on the coast. We had K rations—a piece of chocolate, raisins and things like that. And C rations—tins of M and V, meat and vegetables. You'd chuck those onto the fire, as is. First of all, put a bayonet hole through the top so it wouldn't explode, and then hook it out when you reckoned it was done and fight your way in with a bayonet. We had other food. We must have got a lot of it from the Americans. We didn't starve, that's for sure. There were always coconuts. We'd slice the top off with a machete, bore a hole, drink the coconut juice and eat the flesh inside. The green ones were beautiful drinking. By the way, you never camped under a coconut tree or stayed underneath a coconut tree or put your cot there. A falling coconut could kill you. All through the night you'd hear, Clunk! Clunk! Hitting the sand from 50 feet up.

Can you describe what the jungle is like when you're moving through it?

You usually had someone with a machete, otherwise you couldn't cut your way through it. But in all these islands where natives had been there were well-worn tracks, and normally you would stick to those. The trouble with sticking to a well-worn track is you wonder if the Japs are on the side waiting for you to move through. They sometimes allowed the scouts—the two men in front—to move through. They'd let them go through, and then wait for the body of the troops to come through and attack them from the side with a burst of machine gun and then just disappear into the jungle again, not to be seen. They were good soldiers, the Japanese, fighting for the Emperor, who was revered and had some sort of religious standing in their eyes. It was a shame to be caught as a prisoner of war, and it was no use going home if you'd been a prisoner of war. No one would respect you. With the Japs, you were fighting someone you didn't understand because you didn't understand their philosophy of life.

They wore camouflage suits just the same as we did. We wore camouflage uniform, and you're pretty damn hard to pick in the jungle if you keep your face down. Providing you keep still and shut up and don't have cigarette smoke around.

We caught one Jap in a cave on the side of the coast there. He climbed up inside and a couple of soldiers ran into the cave and shot him. In hindsight I think they might have given him a chance to put his hands up. There were dead Japs on the tracks that we went through, their bodies all swollen. But the Japs were in retreat. From Guadalcanal they were always in retreat. The Battle of Midway, and the Coral Sea, and Guadalcanal, it was the end for the Japs.

> *By June 1944 Harry was back in Guadalcanal receiving medical treatment for hookworm, even though he is convinced he was not infected. He returned to New Zealand on the* **Crescent City**. *After recovering from a hernia operation he was at Papakura Camp waiting for transport to go back overseas when the war ended. After the war he wrote* **Pacific Kiwis**, *a history of 30 Battalion, and taught in secondary schools.*

What sort of impact do you think your war service had on your later life?

It probably sent a message to me that I could cope with my peers. I had been selected from the whole

Cemetery for New Zealand soldiers, Bangaranga, Vella Lavella. ATL, War History Collection, WH-0253

of the battalion to go onto Gizo. I had made a reasonable job of being in the army. I could cope with men, men got along with me well.

I'd never been placed in the position before where I could exercise any confidence. I got on well with my peers—I think I did. I was in the company of some pretty smart men who I recognised as being people to admire. But I didn't feel inferior.

We had to be there in the Pacific, that was our sphere of influence. Curtin, the Prime Minister of Australia, said, 'Bring our troops home.' Darwin had already been bombed. I think in view of the fact that the Americans were moving into the Pacific, they could cope. But we needed to be there to be represented, surely, as a Pacific nation.

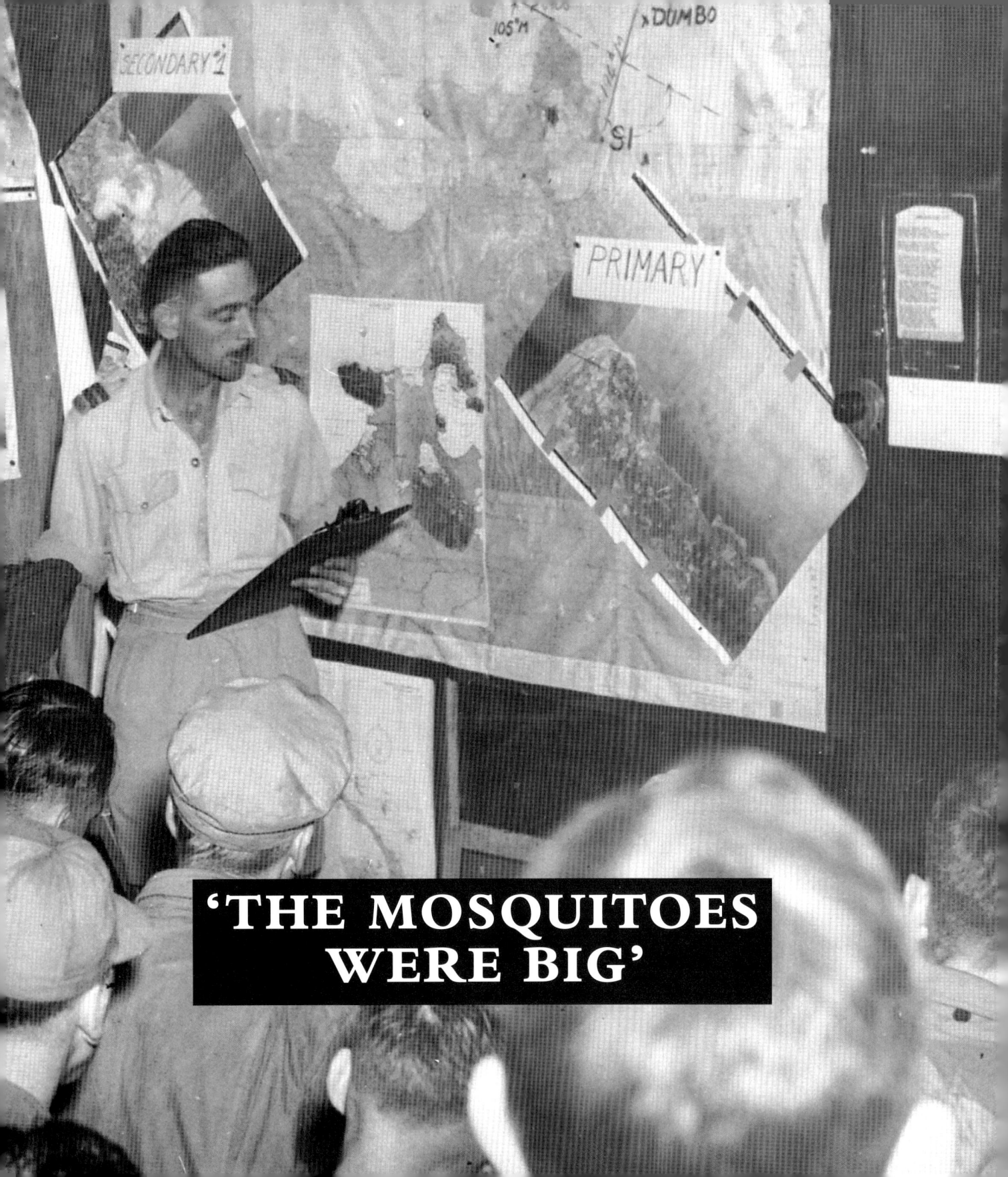

SECONDARY 1

DUMBO

SI

PRIMARY

'THE MOSQUITOES
WERE BIG'

DOUG BENGE, NZ413246, FLYING OFFICER, ROYAL NEW ZEALAND AIR FORCE

Doug Benge was born in March 1920. He was the son of master butcher Thomas Benge, whose shop was well known in Wellington's Aro Street. Although not interested in becoming a butcher, Doug worked in his father's shop from a very young age and remembers that Saturday was very busy because everyone had Sunday roasts in those days. He recalls his feelings when war was declared in 1939.

I WAS TERRIFIED ABOUT IT and the consequences, I remember that quite well. It was then that I decided that I was going to be a pilot. I didn't even consider army life. If it was going to be anything, it was going to be the air force.

I was very disappointed when I could not be accepted as a pilot. It was simply because I did not have two years' secondary education. They said that I could join as neither a pilot nor observer, but I could join as a wireless operator/air gunner—WAG. To begin with, when I was accepted into the air force, I had to do a set of assignments and I went two nights a week to Wellington College. There was an examination after that. The other nights a week I had to go to the Herd Street telegraph station to learn Morse code and keyboard stuff.

When I was accepted into the air force after passing the Wellington College exams and the P & T exams, then I went into ITW, the initial training wing for aircrew, at Levin. That was where everyone—aircrew, wireless operators, pilots—went from civvy street.

Previous page: *An RNZAF briefing before an air strike, Guadalcanal, 1943.* ATL, Evatt Collection, F-106410-1/2
Above: *Doug Benge.* Doug Benge collection

Left: *Benge's butchery in Aro Street, Wellington, in the 1980s.* ATL, J. Sullivan Collection, S-50-120mm-d

Below: *Lockheed Hudsons on Henderson Field, Guadalcanal, 1943.* ATL, J.M. Ellis Collection, F-71947-1/2

What did you do in there?

When I got back to Wellington, I was a very different boy. It was the first time I'd ever had to do what I was told, made to do what I was told. It was tough. The first morning the bugle went and nobody did anything. Didn't get up. Within a week it was a very different thing. They put you out onto the parade ground and put packs on your back. It took about two weeks before we started to do anything, and by that time when the bugle went in the morning, everyone was up and out and dressed. There were English sergeant-major instructors, army people. It was discipline. If the beds weren't made properly, they'd just pull them apart. You'd have to make them again.

After eight weeks at Levin, Doug left for Canada in June 1941 on the Dominion Monarch *for training under the Empire Air Training Scheme. Along with 15 others, he returned to New Zealand after the Japanese attack on Pearl Harbor and was posted to 3 Squadron in Nelson. Doug left for the Pacific at the end of 1942. The squadron was based at Henderson airfield on Guadalcanal, where American Marines had only recently gained the upper hand over the Japanese.*

We flew in, right into the middle of an air attack. We came around the end of the southern part of Guadalcanal and looked up the coast—it was a beautiful day, everything was serene around—but looking up, it looked like a beehive or a hornets' nest. It was black, sort of cone-shaped way up there. It was Henderson Field, and it was under attack from Japanese planes. All we saw were these little dots, as we got closer we could see they were planes. Forty or 50 planes diving. It was a real attack on Henderson Field.

We thought we were getting short on fuel, and there was nowhere else to go. I can remember being really worried then, because we were flying Hudsons. You see, although they were an American plane, they were different from what they'd been using there and the groundcrew wouldn't readily recognise them, and our roundel was on the side. I was worried about trying to get in with this plane. I was standing between the two pilots in the front with the Aldis lamp flashing the letter of the day. Each day you had an identification letter. If you were approaching a ship out at sea, you never went straight at them, you went along the side, you flashed the light until they flashed the light back to you, and then you'd go a bit closer. So I was frantically flashing this.

We just came straight in and landed in amongst the planes everywhere. There were people rushing around, the tyre blew out. We finished up at the end of the runway. The leg folded down, one wing was on the ground.

Suddenly, there in front was a follow-me. They had little open-backed jeeps, along the back of them they had black and white stripes and 'follow me' on it. They'd pick you up at the end of the runway and take you around to your revetment, where you had to park. But instead of this he pulled up in front us and we all piled out and fell into the back, and they rushed us around and we went into a tunnel underneath a mountainous pile of rice sacks, filled with sand. On the top was a very crude radar. The British and the Americans were way ahead of the Japanese as far as radar. It was very crude, though; it looked like a Dutch windmill. We went in a tunnel underneath.

The Americans had only recently taken the airfield from the Japanese.

That was what the trouble was all about—they wanted it back!

The Americans provided new gear for the airmen.

They made us webbing hats with a big brim that came out in the front. They made us shoulder holsters and we were given a .45 automatic—it was a beautiful big gun, it tucked under your arm and felt very comfortable there. And we got a beautiful nylon flying suit, but they were so hot in the tropics.

What did you wear underneath your nylon suits?
Next to nothing. Just skivvies. That was another thing, but you could go to the Marine sergeant-major's big tents where the supplies were, and you could get new issues of clothing, underclothing, every day. A lot of the Americans never washed at all; they just threw them away and got new ones.

Doug recalls the conditions on Guadalcanal.

In the tropics you didn't need very much. At two o'clock in the morning, you might put one sheet on. You didn't adapt to the heat. It was absolutely shocking. The humidity was the trouble. The breeze that was blowing was hot. When I open an oven, I'm back in Guadalcanal. That heat that comes out of the oven, it's exactly like the breeze up there.

We were taking 22 pills a day. A lot of them were salt, but there was Atebrin, too. You went quite yellow with the Atebrin. It didn't stop you from getting malaria, it just made it less dangerous. The mosquitoes were big things, like bees, and they had striped jerseys like the Wellington football jerseys, yellow and black. Although we had mosquito nets and the sides of the tents were always rolled up at night—which wasn't very nice, because you never knew who was out the back there likely to come through—somehow or other these bloody things would get in. They used to get up one end of the net and dive-bomb you—vroom!—down and up to the other end. You had to lie there and wait for it to land on your face and then knock your face off. And if you missed, well, your face still hurt but you hadn't caught him. You couldn't turn any lights on.

Above: *Airmen in the Pacific have a shower*. ATL, Evatt Collection, F-106387-1/2
Right: *Aircrew from 3 Squadron walk away from a Lockheed Hudson, Guadalcanal*. RNZAF Official PR1166, via Air Force Museum, Christchurch

There were Japanese air raids every night.

More or less on the top of this knoll—a big long ridge—was the sergeant-major's tent, and outside that was a big 88-millimetre shell case, hanging on a rope. The Condition Red was Dong, dong! Dong, dong! Dong, dong! Very loud. That meant: get out and get under—do what you can. You could hear the Jap planes at this stage, humming like bees coming in. They'd get louder and louder, and then you'd get this Condition Red. Then on would go the searchlights. They didn't like the searchlights at all. It was like shining a torch in a dark room. You'd pick up a plane. It was just like a moth. Probably at about 25,000 feet, perhaps 20,000 feet. As soon as the searchlights came on, they used to drop their bombs, haphazardly, and it was a matter of luck where you were. There were usually about eight or nine planes, then that'd be over and they'd be gone. Four hours later, at two o'clock in the morning, the same thing again. That happened every night. You didn't have much sleep at all, which was the Japanese plan. At 100°F you couldn't sleep during the day.

There was a shortage of food. They were flying the wounded out and bringing in petrol in 44-gallon drums for the fighters, at this stage. It got quite seriously bad, and our squadron was sent back to New Hebrides because we weren't doing front-line work. Our job was to find Japanese shipping, which we did. They used to come down from the big Japanese base at Rabaul, and shell the place overnight. Our job was to see that they hadn't left Rabaul by 4 p.m., which meant they couldn't be off Guadalcanal that night. It was reconnaissance, straight-out reconnaissance.

On one occasion we spotted a good movement. There were about 14 or 16 Japanese ships that came out from Rabaul, and we saw them from about 14 miles distance. Mostly first you saw whiffs of black smoke coming up from the things, and as you got closer to them you could identify them. They were not far out. So I reported it back to base. As soon as I started reporting, anti-aircraft fire started appearing around because they could hear that we were reporting them. They were listening too.

We turned and headed back towards home, but reported it. We got halfway back and we passed the torpedo bombers and the dive-bombers coming out, a squadron of them. We passed and we waved

our wings. There were quite a number of them. I can remember thinking, I wonder how many of those poor buggers are not going to come back? That was one of the riskiest jobs out.

Doug recalls his feelings about being on operations in the Solomon Islands.

I was right into it, straight away. We were pleased that we weren't doing any mundane things, that we were really into it, but on the occasion we were attacked by six Japanese fighters—one of them whizzed past the plane and you saw that red roundel on it, the red rising sun; when you saw that, you thought, God, this is the real thing. I'm really here. It's a different feeling altogether from training. We only had about 180-mile-an-hour Hudsons and they were flying these Zeros, about twice the speed and manoeuvrability, and there were six of them. If it hadn't been for the fact that there was a bit of cloud cover around, we'd have been cut to pieces. We got into one cloud; we got out; we got into another one, and managed to get away like that. But they'd had a good go at us before that, because when they spotted us we dived. The pilot put it into a very steep dive down onto the water, and I was at the astrodome saying there's one this way and one that way to him, and the pilot was moving the plane around. Turning around, looking out the front, you could see the bullets hitting the water in front of the plane. That's how close we were to the water. Then we levelled out right on the water, and we climbed and snuck into a cloud, and then into another cloud.

Our job was finding shipping. The Japanese soon recognised the routine of patrols we had, and were waiting for us on this faraway leg.

Can you describe to me your position in the plane?

I was in the astrodome. That's in the centre of the plane. You're facing all around, standing, and the turret gunner's right behind you with the four Brownings. If you see a plane coming, you talk to the pilot and he'll either slide the plane left or right as directed from there. That's what I was doing. I had a side-mounted Browning gun, but I was too busy offering directions.

The Hudson was very inferior. You didn't have speed and you didn't have a lot of armament. It was very one-sided. You just had to wait for them to go around and come back and attack you, catch you up. There was nothing you could do to get away.

Our only salvation was the cloud cover.

How long would you fly for at a time?

Four and a half hours, mainly. Five hours at times.

We were very nearly all killed in Kavieng [New Ireland]. We were supposed to have been at 6000 feet taking photographs of a bay. It was a Japanese submarine base. It was a beautiful bay, all lovely green coconut palm trees, but the only thing visible were four Japanese floatplanes moored up along the side of this enormous lagoon open to the sea. That's where the submarines apparently came in, but there were no visible armaments at all, because it was all coconut trees. The situation of the lagoon and the hill meant that if you were making an attack, you had to come in from a certain direction. It was found later that in this area where the planes had to pass through there were massive armaments pointing straight up into the air. They were all controlled from a lookout on the hill.

We made a long, quite steep dive and we opened with the machine guns on the side on the floatplanes. One of them burst into flame. I was in the middle of the aircraft, looking out the window with the Browning gun, and a hole went through the wing, in the middle of the plane,

The capture of the German submarine U 570 by a Lockheed "Hudson" of the British Coastal Command.

PROTECT NEW ZEALAND

BACK THEM UP!
WITH 3% NATIONAL SAVINGS

Poster showing a Lockheed Hudson in action. Note the astrodome at the rear of the aircraft. ATL, Eph-D-WAR-WII-1940/41-1

just to the outside of where I was. An 88-millimetre shell had gone straight through the wing. All the petrol fell out the bottom like a big cloud of white smoke. Hundreds of gallons of fuel just fell out the bottom. The turret gunner called up to the pilot, 'The port motor's on fire.' You see, it looked like smoke. If you look out of an aircraft, the motor is there with a short little exhaust pipe at the bottom. That's always red hot. Well, this one was white hot. The thing I could never understand was how all this fuel passed that and didn't explode. The whole thing should have exploded then, but it didn't.

We were carrying two depth charges, they looked like a 44-gallon drum, and they were set for instant explosion. You could set them to explode on impact, or if you were dropping them against submarines you could drop them so that they sank into the water for one or two seconds before they exploded. Immediately we were hit, the pilot jettisoned these two depth charges. I was standing, and the next thing I knew I was thrown down onto the wooden floor. I got an enormous gash in my left thumb. I was down on my hands and knees in this position for quite a while because of all the g's. We'd started to climb away and to get a bit of height on. When I did get up and look out the astrodome in the middle, I looked back down and there was a gigantic mushroom ring of dust. Sand dust, coming up through the trees. The trees were folding in like matchsticks, as the depth charges had gone whoof! across the top of the ground and cut everything off at the base.

We climbed away and got quite a bit of height on, but we were on one motor. If there'd been any fighters around in the area, we wouldn't have had a chance. We were on full throttle and the engine was getting hotter and hotter, so we started throwing things out. Machine guns, oxygen bottles, anything. We had more than an hour's flying to get back. We were gradually losing height. Anyway, we staggered on, calling up to base, and we couldn't get any reply from them.

In the Pacific you get these areas where you can't contact one base, but someone in another direction can hear you perfectly well—they call them 'skip distances'. So, after getting anxiously onto the base there, and getting no reply from them, a base in New Hebrides replied to me. These were American guys. They had these beautiful big trailers, they wheeled them out and they were a complete radio station. They set them up anywhere. I'd got to know these chaps on the way up to Guadalcanal; I used to spend the evenings with them.

We were in trouble. Shortly after that we'd got through this area and I was able to contact base. We were just above the water. We were getting ready to go in. It was about half an hour before we got to base that another Hudson arrived alongside us, which was a bit of comfort. We staggered back and made a very good landing on one motor, which is always dodgy because you get no chance of going around again. We finished up crossways—a tyre blew out on the landing and we finished across the end of the runway. We were picked up by the jeeps from there.

I was taken off to the Marine hospital, which was big army tents under the coconut groves, and they had a look at my thumb. They got out a thing like a big pepper and salt shaker and they sprinkled something on. It was like a mixture of pepper and salt. This was when penicillin was first invented. It set on my thumb like concrete, and remained like that for about two weeks. They took it off and it was quite all right, came perfectly right. No stitches, no nothing. It was pretty sore. I remember they gave me one of those little miniature bottles of whisky. I kept it for many, many years.

Groundcrew bombing-up a Lockheed PV-1 Ventura, Emirau, 1944. RNZAF Official PR4899, via Air Force Museum, Christchurch

What was the feeling like when you landed?

Well, it was a great relief to be back on ground. You felt like kissing it and pilot Peter Gordon did a very good job to get in. Coming in, there was a little ridge of hills. Just to get over that and then down quickly onto the runway required skill.

Doug recalls that the Japanese were a continuous presence around the camp.

You always slept with your revolver under your pillow. You were backed into the jungle, and there were Japanese in there. They were pretty well subdued, but they used to sneak through and tie bombs on the aircraft. The odd night you'd hear a loud explosion, where they'd blown a plane up. It didn't happen very often, but I can remember two or three occasions.

In January 1943 Doug returned to New Zealand. He trained as a pilot on Tiger Moth aircraft at Taieri, near Dunedin, then undertook a navigation and reconnaissance course in New Plymouth. From there he was posted to Ohakea. In November 1944 Doug started his second tour in the Pacific with 8 Bomber Reconnaissance Squadron, based on Emirau Island.

It was an island similar to Norfolk Island, very much on its own and like a table to land on. I can't recall seeing a native there.

We didn't get out beyond the realms of the airport much, except for one time when we found graves of New Zealand people. We were out one Sunday just fossicking around and we came across a little building. As we approached we came to a wire fence. Going through the gate I found a gravestone and cleared the grass away from the front of it and looked at it, and it was someone from New Zealand, which was flabbergasting. Then we found several others. The only thing I can think of is that I heard of a raider capturing an English-bound liner from Auckland, very early in the war. The passengers were taken off and then the boat was sunk. I haven't heard any more than that. I can only conclude that this is where the passengers were put ashore.

Passengers and crew from the MV Rangitane *were put ashore on Emirau by German raiders just before Christmas 1940.*

There were two or three big American squadrons there, all flying the new Mitchells. They were the first of the tricycle undercarriage, with the wheel in front. They were the planes that were used by Doolittle to bomb Tokyo. We were flying Venturas, American planes.

Doug describes going on bombing raids to Rabaul.

There were nine New Zealanders in three formations of three planes, and possibly 45 American Mitchells flying in similar formations all round. You'd fly over at about 20,000 feet probably, fairly high. You watched the plane in front of you, and when their bomb doors opened, you opened yours, and when their bomb dropped out, you released yours. Six bombs in each plane cover a big area on the ground when dropped simultaneously. The squadron would do this saturation bombing on the airfields to destroy as much as possible to keep the Japanese from using them for flying off and sneaking the odd attacks.

Of course, they had plenty of anti-aircraft ammunition, and you had all this black stuff bursting around here and there. The lead plane, commanded by Wing Commander Salmond of Wellington, was hit in the screen, and the shell went through the roof only inches from his head. The force of the wind blowing through the shatter-proof glass in the windscreen was like sandblasting and blew most of the side of his face away. He was in a very serious condition. He managed to get back, he continued flying—there was nobody else to fly it. The weather was bad and there were 40 or 50 planes in the air. We couldn't see the island when we came back. It was under the storm.

It was like flying alongside a wall, a big black wall which went down to about 500 feet off the floor, then it was all sort of hazy. Little tornadoes would come out of the bottom of the clouds. They looked like rope attached to the cloud, and when they got down to the sea, they would run around in circles all over the sea. There wasn't anywhere else to land. You couldn't see, so it was no good going in. We had to stand off and wait. The storms moved fairly quickly and then after 20 minutes or so, you'd see one end of the island start to appear, then a bit more, then enough to get in. That was fine, as long as you had enough fuel. Quite often you didn't. You'd hear the Americans calling up, 'Jumbo, Jumbo'. That's the Catalinas that pick you up. Several of the bombers always landed in the sea and were picked up. The Jumbos were in the air. If they could spot the downed crew, they could get down close to them and land on the water and pick them up.

On one occasion I had one bomb that was hung up. Only five had gone of the six. I couldn't get rid of it. You had a mechanical device for this problem, an additional manoeuvre where you had to dive and then pull out and then put the manual release on, and that usually forced it down and the bomb releases. But nothing I did would shift it, so I had to close the bomb bays up and notify base that I had a hung-up bomb. They gave me a holding pattern to stay on until they got the other planes in. There were still about 30 or more in the air. The weather conditions were spasmodic—now you could get in and half an hour later you couldn't, sort of thing.

When it was my turn, I got in and landed quite well, and ran up to the end of the runway and was almost stopped when this thing came down in the bay. Big crash. It dropped inside. It wasn't armed at this stage. On the end of the bomb there was a round thing with a fan in it—when the bomb drops this starts the fan up and the fan spins, spins, spins, and then it comes off. Then the bomb is armed. So it was harmless, but it was not a nice feeling to hear this thing drop in the bay. You had to take it in very gently and get out and notify the armourer straight away. They had their means of opening the bay gently and edging the bomb out onto trolleys. But I didn't wait to see that being done!

Doug recalls seeing a crashed plane burning while on Emirau.

That was a shocking thing. Billowing molten fire. No smoke. Just billowing molten fire up high, hundreds of feet. You could feel the heat 200, 300 yards away from it. When it gets hot enough, although the bombs are not fused, they reach a certain temperature and then off they go. Then everything goes off together.

In March 1945 Doug returned to New Zealand.

I was pretty shaky. When I arrived I was sent to Rotorua, which was the convalescent area for the air force. I couldn't hold a cup and saucer in my hand. I used to have to have my meals off the mantelpiece, I was shaking so badly. I couldn't sleep very well, but I soon got over that. I was there for a couple of months. When you got well enough you had the choice of doing certain sports during the day. You could attend gym, or you could do golf or archery. I put my name down for golf, and that's where I got my first golfing lessons. I quickly recovered. Took a few months but then I could hold a cup and saucer.

After a medical examination in Wellington, Doug was passed fit.

I was passed out Fit A. 'A' for reserve officers. I found out recently that I'm still on their reserve A.

With the help of the Brooklyn RSA in Wellington, Doug was able to get a lease-to-buy on a local house, coalyard, cakeshop and bakery. This was a 'dream start' in life for a young man with no money. Twice widowed, Doug now lives near Tauranga with his third wife, Margaret.

Jamie, a US Marine who looked after me on Guadalcanal, always called me 'Lucky Boy'. I guess I still am.

A group of convalescents outside Number 1 Convalescent Depot (Brent's Hotel), Rotorua. RNZAF Official PR3832, via Air Force Museum, Christchurch

'HAWAII'S BEEN ATTACKED'

PETER RENSHAW, 46187,
SERGEANT, 36 BATTALION

Peter Renshaw, the son of Frank and Louise Renshaw, was born in Wellington in 1918. His mother owned a nursing home in Upper Hutt, where Peter grew up. He attended Hutt Valley High School and then studied accountancy. Having joined the Wellington Regiment of the Territorial Force in 1938, he went into camp in 1940. He became engaged to his future wife, Eve Burley, the same year.

I KNEW SHE WAS THE GIRL I wanted to marry. She was a very attractive girl, and we married before I went away in 1941.

What did she think about you going away to the war?
She knew I had to go, because everybody went sooner or later. My mother was upset because she had vivid memories of the First World War when her brother was gassed. She had two brothers who served; one brother was caught in a gas attack. He came home, but he was never in good health and he died. I remember her taking me to see him one day, about 1924. He was in the hospital out of Hastings and he was coughing his heart out. He died a few weeks later. My other uncle, Jack, served with the Australian Army and he came through it all right. I think all of her generation were conscious of the huge casualty lists from the First World War, and she was apprehensive at my going, but she just accepted it as almost inevitable.

His father died when Peter was in camp with the Territorials. In April 1941 he joined the Seventh Reinforcements of 2NZEF and trained at Trentham and Papakura.

Previous page: *New Zealand trucks in New Caledonia about to embark for the Solomon Islands.* ATL, War History Collection, WH-0172
Above: *Peter Renshaw, 1941.* Peter Renshaw collection

Papakura was quite a novelty. It was a nice clean camp, new huts and everything, and we'd get leave to go into Auckland. I'd never been there before. Compared with Wellington it was quite a big city. We'd go to town, and roam around the Auckland streets, take a tram out to the suburbs and ferry over to Devonport, that sort of thing.

So at what stage did you know that you were going to the Pacific?
We had our final leave in November. We were just another reinforcement to go to the Middle East. I met my wife in Christchurch and we had a honeymoon at her place [in Greymouth]. One morning my mother-in-law knocked at the door of the bedroom and said the Japs were in the war. She said, 'Hawaii's been attacked.' I expected to get a message over the radio at any time calling us back to camp, but it didn't happen. We just finished out our leave.

Did you know that when America was attacked it would change things for you?
Oh yes, because Hong Kong was also attacked and Malaya, and we knew that it was all on. There was a great apprehension in the country. I think everybody felt in a vague sort of way that Japan would come in at some stage, but not in the way it happened. Anyway, I finished my leave, went back to camp in Papakura. My wife went back to her job in Wellington. When we got to Papakura there were a lot of strange officers in the camp and we sensed then we weren't going to the Middle East.

Instead, Peter was sent to Fiji, where he served with 2NZEF from January to July 1942, when 3 Division was relieved by the United States 37 Division. He then returned to New Zealand before being sent to Norfolk Island from September 1942 to March 1943.

I think at that stage the battle of Guadalcanal was in the balance. I think the idea was that we were a back-up point or staging area in case things worsened. The 34 Battalion was sent to Tonga. We went to Norfolk Island and had to go ashore in lighters because there was no wharf there. We got ashore and took all our equipment to the camp in the middle of the island. It was primitive, tents. There were few shops on the island, and we were all sort of frustrated and annoyed because we felt we'd been trained as soldiers and here we were stuck on a faraway island. We just trained there. There was nothing much to do. We got to know some of the residents fairly well.

Soldiers practise using boarding nets. ATL, War History Collection, F-20441-1/4

We felt we were just sitting in the backwater, because in the meantime the battle of El Alamein took place and we felt we should be over there. It was very frustrating. We had battery radios, we'd hear the news—BBC news, and news from America. We must have had about the best part of six months there.

What did you do?
Kicked a football around, some chaps went on fishing trips. We'd swim sometimes. We had a boxing tournament, and we'd have concerts, some fellows would sing, that sort of thing. It was very, very, very boring.

> *Peter's unit was then sent aboard the* **President Jackson** *to New Caledonia in preparation for the move to Guadalcanal in the Solomon Islands.*

It was August 1943. About the same time 14 Brigade had left and gone into action in Vella Lavella. Loading and unloading the transport ships was a skilled operation, because the weapons and materials needed first had to be loaded last, and vice versa.

We were loaded on these barges and stopped off for a couple of days at Vanuatu, off Port Vila. We did a practice landing. We had to practise climbing up and down the nets because you had to know what you were doing, and you had to be very careful of your handhold and footholds otherwise you'd go straight to the bottom. One man—I think he was a chaplain—missed his grip and he fell into the boat and badly injured his back. It was lucky he didn't go into the water.

The officers on shore first told us how to do it, put one hand directly over the other going up. It was like climbing up the side of a big building, as you can imagine. When you climbed down to get into the barges you had to time your jump to get in just when the wave was bringing the boat up. If you misjudged your jump you could miss out.

What were your first impressions of Guadalcanal?

It was quite a beautiful island really, lovely greenery. When we got onto Lunga Point, where we disembarked, you could see that the palm trees had been cut down by artillery fire. When we got ashore there were piles of bones. The first night there was an air raid, the Japs came over. They bombed Henderson Field, the American airfield, night after night. The first night an American fighter went up and shot a Japanese bomber down. This was the first time we'd seen a plane shot down. We saw the tracer bullets coming and they caught the bomber. We all let out a cheer.

We had become part of 1 US Amphibious Corps. Wherever you went there'd be bones, sometimes complete skeletons; old uniforms and bits of equipment. We realised how savage the fighting was. Guadalcanal was really a battle that one side or the other had to win to stay in the war.

After about a week, when we'd got our camp established, we were taken out for our landing training to Tulagi Island nearby, and we practised landing on this beach. We were loaded onto destroyers. Ours was the USS *Ward*, which was the first ship to engage the enemy at Pearl Harbor on 7 December 1941. She fired a depth charge at a Jap submarine.

The landing barges would circle around and, after it was signalled, line up and head for the beach. The idea was they'd slam right up on the beach and disgorge their men. We had to practise this until we had it well rehearsed.

Voting in the Pacific in the general election, September 1943. ATL, War History Collection, WH-0135

We were told we were going to land on the Treasury group of islands, which was south of Bougainville. We were told what beach we had to land on and given bearings where the mortars had to fire, and then we had a lecture by a Marine Corps officer. He said, 'We want plenty of prisoners. Prisoners can give us a lot of information.' I'd never seen a Japanese, and he said, 'I've got an interpreter here with me who can give us a lot of information.' He was a Japanese American. He looked evil, a Japanese, but he was just an ordinary American.

What was the general feeling among New Zealanders towards the Japanese at that stage?
One of hatred. They'd committed terrible atrocities by this time, which had filtered back. They did some terrible things.

Now, there was a general election while you were there?

Yes, in 1943. We voted on Guadalcanal. There was a tent set up as a polling booth, you went in and cast your vote the same as you would do in New Zealand.

Was there someone who was most popular amongst the troops in terms of the possible Prime Minister?

The general feeling was that Peter Fraser was doing a good job. The Labour government was still very popular. I don't know whether there was any general perception, but I think most people felt that he was a leader, the man to take us along.

How did it feel voting in a New Zealand election up there?

It did seem rather odd.

Peter's unit was leaving for Mono Island, further north in the Solomons.

Kiwi troops apply camouflage before going into action. ATL, War History Collection, WH-0808

Before we went into action we had camouflage dye to rub over our faces. Green dye. You looked like a sort of a gargoyle. It came in a bag, you mixed it up with a bit of water and smeared it over your face. We did this to each other. Just smeared all around your ears and neck. We could hardly recognise each other.

We got up early in the morning. We had camouflage jungle suits—a camouflage grey khaki suit, different patterns, grey and brown patches. They weren't very comfortable. We had heavy cleated jungle boots.

We were all tensed up, and I don't suppose anybody slept that night. We got up early in the morning and went down to the beach. Most of the people had their camouflage and dye on by this time. Whole of 8 Brigade—about 5000, I suppose.

All the insignia and rank had to be taken off, the officers' pips and sergeants' chevrons. And you weren't allowed to address officers by rank in case the Japs overheard, they might know someone was an officer. Our officer said to us before, 'You can call me Tom. If you want to write a final letter home, give it to me. I'll see it gets home.' So we all sent a final letter home.

Peter wrote to his wife.

I think they all knew back home that we were going into battle.

How did you travel up to Mono from Guadalcanal?

On a destroyer, USS *Ward*. We must have left in the early afternoon. The slower ships left earlier. I remember I slept up on deck, which was a silly thing to do because it was pretty rough, it was pitching around and I could have gone overboard. I lay there and tried to keep still, and I must have dozed off. In the early hours of the morning I heard this almighty roar—the escorting warships had opened up and were plastering the beach. It was quite a big operation. Then we were given the order to get on board the barges. The barges set off, and then shortly the Japs on the shore opened up on us and we could hear bullets whizzing past. I thought, Gee, when the ramp comes down you don't know what's going to happen.

When I was on the barge waiting to go ashore—it sounds funny, but I could picture my mother and I thought I could see her bending over me. She had her nurse's white uniform on, a nurse's cap, and she

On board a destroyer in the Pacific. Harry Bioletti collection

was smiling at me. It sounds almost bizarre, but I had that feeling. It was weird. I never told her about it afterwards, but I suppose I should have. I've thought about it quite a lot since.

When the ramp came down, you saw that you could be hit. Some of the fellows on the bigger ships, the LSTs [landing ship tanks], never got ashore. Some of them were killed and they never fired a shot. You had your rifle beside you, you were hunched up, very tense. A horrible feeling. I thought, When the ramp comes down I'm going to cop it, but I didn't.

When we hit the shore it was different from what we experienced in our training, it was quite stony. We got ashore anyway. We landed right up on the beach. We all piled out, got the mortar set up and unloaded the bombs. The gunfire and the din were almost more than you could bear. You don't think too much that you might be killed. You just do what you've got to do.

They were still firing at you?
Not by that time, no. But of course we didn't know what was going on further along. There was quite a

An LST. This one is landing a bulldozer on Nissan Island. ATL, War History Collection, F–44750-1/2

lot of action further along. We got the mortar set up and started firing, and then the other troops landed. It was all confusion from that point onwards.

There was one Jap machine gun dug in on the beach and, as I recall the story, one of the Americans came ashore from one of the LSTs on a bulldozer and he dropped his blade and scooped these people up, buried them alive.

Japanese prisoners, Mono Island. Drawing by Russell Clark. Archives New Zealand, AAAC 898, NCWA 134

Did you see that happening?

No, you didn't see much of what went on in an actual battle. You heard about things later on, but you realise that your own involvement is so small. It seems important to you, but it's only part of the operation. You're just a cog in a big wheel, and it has to be that way.

I think there were about 40 of our brigade killed in the first couple of days, and quite a lot of wounded. The worst of the wounded were taken off and sent back to Guadalcanal. The dead we just buried on the beach. It was quite a critical landing because it paved the way for the attack on Bougainville by 3 Marine Corps division. Falamai Beach, that's where we landed. Our battalion had the most casualties.

Why was the first night the worst part?

Some of the Japs infiltrated through our lines; several were killed. After the first night I suppose the resistance was broken and the worst of it was over. We sent out patrols around the island to try to catch the rest of the Japs. Some had retreated to the other side of the island and they were caught by another force that had landed over there. They were all killed, I think.

Sometimes you could hear things. Your imagination would run away with you. Sometimes fellows would think they heard something and they'd cut loose with a shot, you know, and in the morning we'd talk about it. You wouldn't sleep, you'd be tensed up all the time. You might doze off. Land crabs, huge crabs, would come out of the coral and scratch around. They were horrible things.

What noises did you hear?

These big land crabs scratching around; there'd be sirens going when an air attack was expected; guns going off all the time, because the anti-aircraft guns would be shooting. We could hear the bombers overhead, sometimes they'd come in and cut their engines, just drift down. You wouldn't know where they were, but you'd sense them right above.

How did that affect people?

You were trained for it, you just accepted it. The fitter you were, of course, the better you coped with it. One or two people, I think the strain got to them. I didn't really become aware of that until we went back to 4 General Hospital in New Caledonia. There were several people who cracked under the strain, from different units. They got shaky and weren't much good.

When you were on Mono, did you see any Japanese?

Only a few dead ones.

After a few days I got very sick. I knew there was something pretty badly wrong with me, I didn't know what it was at the time. I started to feel very sick. There was quite a bit of malaria, but not as acute as it was with the Americans, and a lot of people got hepatitis like I did. You couldn't have a proper wash, and you might pick up dirt when you were eating.

I was so sick I didn't care whether I lived or died, so I went along to the RAP and the doctor said, 'I'll send you over to the field ambulance in Stirling Island.' He thought I might have hepatitis, which I did. I had to hand my rifle in and ammunition, grenades, and then I was taken to Stirling. It was a big marquee and there were Americans and New Zealanders there. I was there for a few days and met several Americans. Some were badly wounded. I remember one big boy from Mississippi, and he spoke in this sort of drawling American accent. He was very sick. A lot of the Americans got malaria. They wouldn't take their Atebrin tablets because they thought they would make them sterile.

After a few days I was sent to Guadalcanal to the Kiwi casualty station there. I'd lost an awful lot of weight. I was just skin and bone. I only had a few days in Guadalcanal, then I was sent back to the base hospital in New Caledonia, and I was there for a few weeks. We went out on trips to Noumea, and after a while I was sent up to the convalescent depot, not very far from Bourail. We'd swim and we had to do a lot of exercise, but I still couldn't put on any weight and the doctors were puzzled.

Patients' recreation room, 4 NZ General Hospital, New Caledonia, 1943. Kathleen Hogg collection

I was so skinny. I think I picked up a bit in health, then I went to the medical board and I was sent home. I did pick up when I got home, back to civilian life.

What other conditions were people in the hospital with?
Exhaustion; some of the people were wounded, of course. One chap had lost his arm. Various medical complaints, hepatitis. It was a New Zealand hospital. But we were adjacent to an American hospital. They would come over sometimes, there was quite a bit of contact. We'd go and see films.

Did you have any difficulties in those post-war months with nightmares or anything like that?
Sometimes my mind would be in a whirl. It seemed to me not fair that life was so normal back home when fellows were fighting and dying overseas. I would have come back about March 1944, I think. There seemed to be such a lot of complacency back home and it just didn't seem to be fair.

Sister M.S. Farland and patients, 4 NZ General Hospital, New Caledonia. Archives New
Zealand, WAII, 7/6, L1 613/21, 553

I felt that we should have been given more consideration. By that time a lot of us had come back,
you see. With the manpower circumstances as they were at the time, a man accompanied by a policeman
could walk into a hotel lounge and pick on people and say, 'Why aren't you working?', and the policeman
would pick him up. He could take your name and address and you'd be in trouble. You wore your RSA
badge everywhere. It meant that people recognised you'd been away.

What about service in the Pacific? Do you think that that was recognised?
I don't think it has been. I don't think people realised what we'd done, you know. Mono was actually
the first opposed landing by New Zealanders since Gallipoli. It was a tough one, people didn't realise
that. I suppose we expected to be recognised for what we'd done, and we felt we weren't.

I used to bump into my old mates, and we sometimes used to drink in the old Grand Hotel in Willis
Street [in Wellington]. We'd talk about where we'd been and that sort of thing, and we all had this

feeling that we should have been given more recognition.

I always felt I should have gone away earlier and seen more of the war. But you went where you were sent; you did what you were told to do. Most of the men in my battalion went to Italy later.

What are your feelings towards the Japanese today?
I've met several and my daughter had some staying as exchange students, and they were very nice teenagers. Nice, well-mannered boys and girls. If you start talking about the war, they probably wouldn't even know what you were talking about.

So your feelings about being involved in the war, what are they today?
I wouldn't have missed it, because of the comradeship and the feeling of being able to say I was there. I think a lot of the bodies I saw wrapped up on the beach at Mono. Young men who, if they'd lived, would have been grandparents now like I am, great-grandparents. That's just life. It wasn't fair. You cast your mind back over years when you get older, and you think about a lot of things and you realise you're lucky to be alive. So many good men went away and never came back. And there were so many fit, Grade 1 men who could have gone and didn't. That was why when the men from the Middle East returned home in the furlough drafts they mutinied and refused to return. You couldn't blame them.

'RIDING BEAUTIFUL
MOTORBIKES'

ROB McLEAN, 139764,
LANCE CORPORAL, 5 PROVOST COMPANY

Rob McLean was born in Christchurch in 1921. His father Alexander had served in the First World War. Rob grew up in Lyttelton and worked as a warehouseman and salesman for the firm of Ross & Glendining after leaving school. In 1940 he was called up to serve in the war.

EVERYBODY IN NEW ZEALAND, soon as they turned 19, received a letter in the post. You were called up. I was posted to 5 Provost Company.

What did you know about the Provosts?

Nothing. I went to ask people, 'What's this Provost business?' 'Oh gosh, you want to get out of that, it's terrible. No, don't be in that. People don't like you.' It's a fundamental thing of New Zealand males, I suppose. They don't like authority and so they don't like Provosts, just because of that. I mean, we were just ordinary folks, the same as them, called up the same as them, shoved into it.

I didn't want to be in a unit that wasn't very popular, but as it turned out it was the most wonderful thing that could happen to me, because my mother and father wouldn't allow me to have a motorbike. Lo and behold, I ended up in 5 Provost Company, which is a motorcycle traffic control unit of the army, riding beautiful motorbikes. It was paradise.

Previous page: *A three-ton truck in a ditch near Moindou Pass, New Caledonia.* ATL, War History Collection, F-20436-1/4
Above: *Rob McLean in 1940 in Territorial uniform.*
Rob McLean collection
Right: *5 Provost Company training at Burnham, 1941.*
Rob McLean collection

Rob trained at Burnham Camp and was then posted overseas, arriving in New Caledonia in October 1942.

We operated attached to other units, but not part of them. Our job in New Caledonia was to control the traffic. We had a pretty tricky job because the roads were only built for Renault cars and maybe five trucks a year. There was one road that went from the bottom to the top, a one-lane road down the east side. The road was being cut up by the big six-wheel, five-ton American trucks which our boys were using. And so the Provosts had to stop all that and get them down to a certain speed. It's a wonder I wasn't killed there, rather than anywhere else, because a truck would belt past you and you'd have to chase this fella and either give him a ticket or give him a warning. But to pass them was a real ordeal, because it was a shingle road and not that wide.

Rob McLean (left) and his friend Gordon Grigor in a creek near Moindou Pass, New Caledonia, 1943.
Rob McLean collection

They had to stop. One of our boys, he pulled up the Brigade Major in his command car. He was speeding. Gordon Grigor it was, he was a friend of mine. To pull up the major! I think our captain told him off about it.

We also had our good times too, mind you, because being a motorcycle unit with our own agenda, more or less, our officers would say, 'What say we go for a trip over to the other side of the island?' So away we'd go over to the other side, and tour round and see people. It was different altogether. Beautiful trees, tropical. It was lovely. We got to know a family over there, French, and they had a daughter. She was real nice. Of course, we were all young and interested in any girls. One of my friends, he was a very attractive fella, he was the only one that got anywhere near her. We didn't.

We went on another trip overland to a nickel mine. We tootled over there and had a look. They had Javanese people from Indonesia working on the mine. I gave a man a gift and he said, 'You've been very, very kind. I'll give you my wife.' They were living in little wee hovels built of corrugated iron and that sort of thing, but inside it was absolutely spotless. Everything was clean. Quite a lot of children. She was right there in front of me. I didn't know whether he was giving her to me just for sexual reasons or to take her away. She just stood there. I've forgotten what I gave him—might have been a tin of meat or something like that.

When I went to school, I learnt French. Only for two years, but I liked French. I really enjoyed it and I got reasonable at it, so when we landed there it was the best thing I ever did. I ended up in a French colony. The boys who didn't learn French never ever got to be able to communicate, but I was able to communicate in a sort of a way with these local French people.

Rob was posted to the Moindou Pass in New Caledonia to direct traffic for a couple of months. After his stint there, Rob returned to Divisional Headquarters. He remembers how the men spent their leisure time.

I think we used to get a beer ration; we got New Zealand beer. Some of the chaps didn't drink, so they'd give us their ration. We used to save it up till the end of the week, then we'd have a bit of a session. I'd play the harmonica: 'Irish Eyes Are Smiling', 'Roll Out the Barrel', all old songs like that which the boys could bellow out when they got really drunk. It was real good fun. Nobody had any other instruments. You can imagine us sitting around in a tent, all bellowing it out. There'd be about 15 people in a tent, all crowded in.

In 1943 Rob and his Provost unit left New Caledonia for Guadalcanal in the Solomon Islands.

We called in at New Hebrides, and at the Vila harbour we did a landing training exercise. We were on a big ship and so to get us ashore they threw rope netting down the side of the ship. We had to climb down with a full pack on, rifle, and helmet, the works. It was pretty tough going, because the thing was swaying.

You got onto a landing barge and then we landed on the beach. Then we had to go inland and consolidate ourselves there. We didn't do anything. Normally the Provosts' job is to be one of the early ones landing, so when we got there we were supposed to direct some of the other barges to different places. The Americans did it differently. Their system was that the barges would hit the beach, they'd pour out of them, and start firing and advance inland. Maybe 100 metres, 200 metres. The next wave would do the same and shoot half of their own men from the first lot. I was told about it. They had a reputation for being trigger-happy. When we were on guard on stores dumps, we had to be mighty careful. If you were to take over from them, you were lucky to get there in one piece, because you had to come along at night-time to take over from them, and you were liable to get shot because they'd shoot anybody.

Rob recalls landing on Guadalcanal.

When I landed there I realised I was in the war. There wasn't a shred of leaf on the trees. All you saw was trunks of trees all the way back from the beach from the shelling that went on there. There were thousands of American soldiers killed, and they were nearly pushed off there by the Japs. There were a few sunken wrecks of ships about here and there. We landed in barges. It was hard work, carting all the stores and ammunition and everything out of the barges, onto the shore, into trucks and away to different camps. Everybody just had to turn in and cart stuff. It was very hot. Nobody wore many clothes. They wore trousers. You never wore anything on top.

Did you have any sense of fear at that stage?
No. But I did get a bit of a shock when I saw all those jolly trees with no leaves on, trunks blown off. It was all interesting. At that age you think it's all interesting. You don't get worried about it.

The control post at Moindou Pass. ATL, War History Collection, F-44806-1/2

Provost Company and 35 Battalion with artillery on Vella Lavella. Rob McLean collection

I think we were only there for about a month. We were living in tents there for a short time before we moved up to Vella Lavella.

We weren't the initial assault landing, so we landed from barges and came ashore and set up. Then they divided us up into two sections. 14 Brigade section and 8 Brigade section. We were attached to the 35 Battalion assault group. That was up the western side. We were around on the eastern side, so we went by barge right up there.

We came ashore and then we had to dig our foxholes. It was hard digging, but it wasn't too bad because we were about 50 or 60 metres inland, in from the beach, in the jungle. That's where we spent our time for the next couple of months.

Rob had landed at Maravari on Vella Lavella, and then his unit was moved to Pakoi Bay on the west coast.

We were guarding the 14 Brigade headquarters. The Japs could come in through the jungle, and I thought, The Japs could come in on us at night-time if the guards don't spot them, so I went into the jungle and got all this jungle lawyer. It's a creeper. I spread it about 20 metres or so in front of our foxholes. I went to a lot of trouble, so that anybody who was coming in from that direction would get caught up in this lawyer. You can't get rid of it, it just attaches itself onto you.

One of the worst aspects wasn't the Japs coming in onto us—well, it was. Yes, that was the worst. But the second worst was the land crabs. They were murder. They'd be a luncheon-plate size, sort of a pinky colour, and they had a salty smell. Over there, as soon as the sun goes down, boom! It's dark. We were 50 or 60 metres in from the beach, and you could hear them coming from there. Rustle, rustle, rustle, crunkle, crunkle, crunkle. Thousands of these crabs coming out of the sea onto the land. It was quite noticeable, the noise that they made creeping along.

How could you keep them out of your foxholes?
You couldn't. They'd crawl in on top of you. You'd wake up and there'd be a salty smell—it wasn't such a bad smell—but the salty smell of this crab on your face wasn't much good. They nipped you. I used to dread the night because of them.

One of the Provosts' jobs on Vella Lavella was to guard Japanese prisoners.

There were four of them. We had to guard them in a wee hut made of grass, with a grass roof. We had to tie their hands behind their back and strip their clothes off them. We had to make sure they didn't have any armaments on them. They were in a pair of shorts in this hut, hands tied behind their back, because the trouble was they'd make a go at you so that you'd have to shoot them. That's what they wanted. Being taken prisoner was one of the biggest disgraces, and so they weren't happy. They'd try to make a go for you so that you would possibly shoot them and then they would go to the Japanese heaven. They had to sit on the ground, you had to see that they sat down on the ground. They weren't saying much to each other. They were pretty sad. The Intelligence people took them over. At various times they'd take one away and interrogate him and then bring him back and get another one, and so forth. We weren't giving them food. Intelligence fed them. I think they were only there for about three days, and then they were taken away south.

The food that the Provosts ate was army fare.

We were on C rations. For breakfast we'd have oatmeal. There'd be a little plastic sachet of oatmeal and a little sachet of powdered milk. You had your mug, so you'd mix up the oatmeal with the powdered milk and water, and that'd be your breakfast. And there might be a couple of biscuits to go with it.

Then at midday you'd open another tin, and that'd probably have powdered lemon drink. We used to have tinned beans and biscuits and lemon powder. For dinner, we had hash—we had a lot of hash. We had hash of meat and dehydrated potatoes, dehydrated carrots. They didn't really taste much like a real potato. But there was dessert. We'd have some custard powder, which we'd mix up with water and some dried apricots, those sort of things. Everything was cold, we never had anything hot. We never had a hot meal for months. You got sick of it, the same old thing for breakfast, dinner, and tea.

After about a month at Pakoi Bay, Rob returned to Divisional Headquarters at Gill's Plantation.

After the Japanese engagement had finished and they'd driven them off the island, we had to spend about six months there. Everybody started making things or doing things. We'd all have some sort of racket where you could sell something to the Yanks and prise a bit of money off them. They had heaps of money, they were loaded. What we wanted to do was get some of the money off them.

Charlie Wallace and I made ornaments. We used to raffle them. We used to go down to the PX club. We had a notebook and wrote down everybody's number and drew the thing off. We were raking in the money, charging an American dollar per ticket.

What sort of things were you making?
We used to make ashtrays and little trinkets and brooches cut out of brown coconut wood. It's very nice, lovely and shiny. I never used shells.

Rob recalls the activities of a friend of his in another Provost unit.

They ran whisky-stills in the jungle. It was illegal, but they used to have them hidden in the jungle and make it [the whisky] out of tins of fruit and that sort of thing. The Americans used to drink a lot of whisky. They used to make very good quality whisky, but sometimes, if they didn't allow it to go right through the whole process, it used to end up as sort of jungle juice. I remember some Americans went blind when they drank it. Somebody or other made it badly. They used to sell it for a fair amount of money.

In 1944 Rob's unit was sent north to the Green Islands.

I didn't know where we were going. All I knew was that we were going to another island to drive the Japanese off, but I didn't have a clue where it was. We went with 14 Brigade aboard an infantry landing craft. It wasn't the type where the big doors go down and you go off and wade through the water onto the beach. It had platforms that went down each side of the bow, so you went aboard that way. We came from our camp with our gear, and went aboard about five o'clock. We were to leave at dawn the next day. I suppose there'd be about 500 of us in that group.

They put up a big screen on the deck and played a movie there. I thought we would be up against Japanese opposition. I was a wee bit nervous about that.

The movie was **Stormy Weather,** *with the famous song of the same name sung by Lena Horne.*

I presume that the army put it on to take our minds off the landing. To me it didn't do that at all, because all I could do was sit there and listen—I couldn't even tell you what the movie was about—but all I knew was that Lena Horne was singing this music. I was worrying about how I was going to get on the next day and whether I'd be still around. That tune, every time I hear it, I can remember sitting on the deck there, not talking to anybody. Most of the other fellas were much the same. They were just sitting, nobody was actually talking and laughing much.

When we were coming in towards Nissan Island we were in a convoy. Most of the big barges were towing a balloon, but we didn't have one to stop dive-bombers diving down onto us. We were attacked by two Japanese dive-bombers. They came in and aimed themselves straight at us. I was on the deck, I was looking up and I could see darn near into the pilots' eyes as they were coming down. They missed us. One plane dropped their bombs on one side of the ship and the other one dropped them on the other side. Then they veered away. But our New Zealand anti-aircraft gunners were on the deck and were firing at them. They were hammering away. I was right beside this gun and it was absolutely painful, so loud I thought it'd burst my eardrums. As they came into sight and started diving down, I thought, This'll probably be the end. But I stood and watched. It was all over in a flash.

We landed there, stopped there for a day and then moved on around [to the south of the island]. The whole island was pretty well all coconut palms, 30 feet high. The undergrowth was six foot high.

We had to be on guard every night. You get a bit nervous, so you walk carefully and try to listen, because you never know how close a person can be in scrub. A person can be very close and if they're not moving, you won't know they're there. Once we knew there was no Japanese in our area, we could talk to each other and do what we wanted to do.

When we first came around Nissan, we didn't know how we were placed with the Japs. We didn't know if they'd been cleared from that area. We had to be careful then. There was 30 Battalion and another battalion. The infantry battalions cleared them off, apart from a few strays they missed. When we first landed we only had pup tents in the jungle for maybe two to three weeks. Then we moved around the island.

We had to help round up the native people who had been on Nissan and Vella Lavella for some years. The Japs had not given them any medical supplies at all, and so they were in very bad health. Some of them were really bad, great big ulcers all over their bodies. Most of them had malaria, of course, and they had hookworm, and some of them had elephantiasis. There were some children. The medical unit sorted them out, so we had to escort them back through the jungle to the barge which would take them back to Guadalcanal, to hospital.

Did they seem willing to go with you?
Yes, they did. Well, they didn't refuse to go. They seemed to know we were caring for them.

Rob recalls coming across some of the Japanese troops who were still on the island.

I explored around. Nissan is just a coral circle, a round circle reef with an entrance into a lagoon in the middle. Only a narrow strip, three kilometres wide, but it's got big steep cliffs on the seaward side. There were caves around there, and myself and my mate went into the caves. The Japs must have heard us coming because they took off out.

In one cave there was still a fire going.

You could smell they'd been there, because they smell differently to us and it was quite noticeable, but there was nobody there.

One of my friends lost some of his washing off the line. The Japanese who were still living in the jungle pinched his clothing, or some of it. That used to occur from time to time. And I remember the case, too, where somebody went to the toilet, and one of his friends had been there already and he was sitting there with a bullet hole right through his head. Some Japanese must have killed him.

The heat and the insects and the disease were just as big a threat to us as the bombs and Japanese.

A medical officer treats a child on Nissan Island. ATL, War History Collection, F-41783-1/2

We had to take Atebrin tablets every day and they made you go all yellow. They didn't stop you getting malaria, they stopped the malaria showing up. Basically the army didn't have a casualty: they had a person, a soldier, who had malaria, but he was still on the job. The army did have a very high degree of hygiene. Every time we washed our dishes, they had to be put into boiling water to be sterilised, and if you didn't do it, you'd be told off. There was other regulations too—one was you were never allowed to go around in bare feet, because you would get hookworm out of the soil. The natives were full of hookworm because they had bare feet.

New Zealanders on a beach at Nissan Island. ATL, War History Collection, WH-0491

Did you have any problems with your skin?

Everybody did. You got rashes. I got prickly heat, which I had for about six months after I came home. It's a rash, a sort of a subterranean rash. Prickly, as if there's a lot of needles going into you, all over you. It can be on every part of your body. It's like ten million needles. It took a while to get out of the system. Once you were in a cool climate, it disappeared.

Did you ever get any coral sores?

Yes, I did. Festery sores. Everything festered, I noticed, up there. I did get shingles. I wondered what it was. I was sore right around my waist, about my belt level. It was shingles. They just rubbed calamine on it like they did with everything else. The RAP, Regimental Aid Post, they must have gone through gallons of that.

Did you have any contact with US troops on Nissan?

We got on well with them. We used to have some great old chats with the Americans on Nissan, because there were more Americans there than other places. They wouldn't have a clue where New Zealand was. They were good blokes, I suppose.

The people that I was up there with—some were mean and selfish, and others were generous and friendly and couldn't do enough for you. I can remember those people so well, and I cherish their memories because I was living with them, sleeping with them in the same tents, and doing all the same things with them. Those people, they are the thing that I would put down as number one. The Provost company. They were all different from each other, but I did get a lot from them, and I suppose they got a bit from me, too.

Your feelings about the time spent serving in the Pacific—do you feel it was worthwhile?

Oh yes, very much so. In fact, I feel that the 3 New Zealand Division was actually on the doorstep, defending New Zealand. There wasn't much publicity about the Pacific War. All the publicity seemed to be about the European side, so the people didn't know much about it.

And what are your thoughts on war in general now?

I think it's a very bad thing. If they could only just talk to each other and solve it that way.

After his return from the Pacific in 1944, Rob served in Italy.

It was totally different. It was sort of on a worldwide scale, whereas in the Pacific it was more of an individual thing. Closer, smaller numbers of people. In Italy, large numbers. Thousands. All attacking at the same time. Big numbers, bigger operation.

When we went from the Pacific to the 2 Division, they didn't have a very high opinion of us. They thought we were a bunch of coconut bombers, sitting under coconut trees, just lapping up the sun. That was their attitude. People had the wrong idea.

'WE STARTED
TO FLOOD'

JAMES MURPHY, NZD1188, CHIEF PETTY OFFICER, ROYAL NEW ZEALAND NAVY

James Murphy was born in Devonport, England, on 28 October 1910. His family emigrated to New Zealand and went to live in Bluff, where his father served as a policeman. In January 1933, Jim joined the Royal Navy at Devonport in Auckland.

I SAW SOMETHING IN THE LOCAL PAPER about the navy and that there were New Zealanders in it too. I can't remember how I found out, but I wrote away to the officer in charge of the naval base in Auckland, and about six weeks later they replied to say that they were going to send me a free ferry and train warrant to go to Auckland to see if I was suitable. And to see if I could pass the entrance exams.

I was up there early January [1933] in order to do these things, and I lived aboard HMS *Philomel*, which had been decommissioned and was used purely as base accommodation and a training ship. Some of the machinery had been taken out of her and she was tied up to the wharf. That was the headquarters in Auckland.

How did you find navy life when you first joined?

I was terribly homesick. And it was some weeks before I knew that I was accepted. I had to sign up for 12 years, and went through military training and swimming tests in the dock. The swimming test was to dive or jump in off the caisson—that's the dock gate that keeps the water in or out—and swim the length of the dock. I was told to undress and given a pair of overalls which were about three sizes too big for me, and they said I could dive or jump in. I wasn't very good at diving so I jumped, and these

Previous page: *Sailors on HMS* Leander *take a break, 1941.* ATL, Evening Post Collection, G-49238-1/4
Above: *Jim Murphy.* James Murphy collection

things were flapping around my legs, but I managed to get to the other end. I was never very fast but I could last a long time, and I thought, Well, if you're going to go overboard in the middle of an ocean, speed doesn't matter much as long as you can stay afloat. And I practised floating so that I could float for a long time. When you got tired you could float.

After training, Jim was posted to the cruiser HMS **Diomede** *with the rank of engine room artificer, fifth class.*

If I did what I was told, and I had to do written homework as well, and they were satisfied, then I was elevated to fourth class, acting. I was given assignments to do every week, written assignments—questions

HMS Diomede *at Nelson, c. 1932.* ATL, F.N. Jones Collection, G-12658-1/2

and answers, drawings of different parts of the machinery, and so on. If that was satisfactory, then at the end of 12 months I was confirmed fourth class.

I went down into the engine room as an extra person in training, and when I saw the maze of machinery and steam pipes, water pipes, electrical fittings and everything else, valves that had to be opened and shut at different times, and the control valves, called manoeuvring valves, and the machines for making fresh water, and so on, I looked around and I thought, I'll never know what happens here and what to do and how to find out. I was with a very broadly spoken Irishman, and as soon as I'd ask him a question he'd say, 'The best way to find out is follow the pipeline overhead or in the bilge until you find the answer.'

There were just the two of us in that engine room. The ship had two engine rooms, and there was another artificer in the other engine room. They were called the forward and aft engine rooms.

What does 'artificer' mean?

It means skilled in some particular trade or practice. Besides the artificer there were two or three stokers. The ship used oil fuel. We had turbine main engines with reciprocating auxiliary machinery.

> *Jim served on* **Diomede** *until 1936, when he joined HMS* **Achilles,** *on which he sailed back to New Zealand from England. He was serving on HMS* **Leander** *when war was declared.* **Leander** *escorted the Second Echelon of the New Zealand Division, which was diverted to England while en route to Egypt.* **Leander** *itself went to Egypt and continued duty in the Middle East before being sent to the Pacific theatre. He was on board* **Leander** *when it was hit by a torpedo during the naval engagement at Kolombangara in the Solomon Islands in July 1943.*

Tell me about the battle of Kolombangara.

Intelligence told us that Japanese were bringing down troops on fast destroyers because the troopships were being sunk, and they were losing too many. The destroyers would come down loaded up with troops, escorted by one or two cruisers. It was called the 'Tokyo Express'. We left our anchorage further south and went up two nights but didn't meet anybody. The third night they came in sight on the radar at about one o'clock, about 20 miles away. They were doing about 25 knots and we were doing about 25 knots, so we were approaching each other at well over 50 miles an hour. That's closing in pretty fast.

Jim Murphy (right) in the engine room of HMS Leander. James Murphy collection

When we got within range we started firing, and so did they. We were quite close then. There were guns firing and torpedoes tracking everywhere.

Where were you?

I was in the forward engine room. We were speeding and changing direction, heeling over as we altered course to avoid other ships, because it was fairly close range. All this firing was going on, and the chaps up top reckoned it was really spectacular, because the Yanks were firing tracers. There were star shells if you wanted to light up the sky, armour-piercing shells, all sorts. Then suddenly there was an almighty muffled bang, not a sharp one. The ship shook as though there was a severe earthquake, and then we started to list to port.

We got it on the port side between the foremast and the funnel on the only armour-plated bulkhead in the ship, which split the explosion. Otherwise it could have cut us in half. The four-inch armour plating on the ship's side may have helped to reduce damage.

The torpedo from a Japanese destroyer hit **Leander** *at quarter past one in the morning.*

The engineer commander was standing near me. We both said the same thing: 'What the hell is that?' He said, 'I'm going to see what's what, chief', so he disappeared up the engine ladder to gain first-hand knowledge.

The shake shook all the dust off the asbestos-lagged steam pipes overhead, and then some smoke came down through the supply fan and I thought we were on fire too, but it wasn't that. It was just the smoke from the general battle. In wartime we steamed in units. Each engine had its own set of boilers, so if one unit was affected it didn't affect the others. I saw the gauges drop, so I knew there was something wrong in A boiler room. That's the first one from the bow of the ship. It was out of action. Then we lost pressure in B boiler room. The dynamos aft were OK; the forward dynamos were dead and that half of the ship was in darkness. Repair parties quickly rigged power cables as we'd practised many times.

Did you have light?

Yes, because we were in the stern half of the ship, and we had dynamos aft of us. They were in units, too. In peacetime *Leander* just had two dynamos running when at sea, but in wartime all four dynamos were connected. Then we started to flood in the forward engine room, and we didn't know where it was coming from because so many systems had been upset. It was a mixture of salt water, oil and hot water, and we eventually found out where it was and corrected that. The starboard bilge pump was high and dry because of the ship's list to port. The port bilge pump was on the point of being put out of action because of the rising floodwaters. So we used the main inlet, which could draw water from the bilge instead of from the sea. That main inlet supplied salt water, which was pumped through the condenser tubes to change exhaust steam back into water, which was then pumped back to the boilers.

They got the engines going after about five minutes.

We had to stop them to conserve steam, as our only boiler room still operating seemed to be losing pressure, and we needed to preserve steam for our dynamos. We got the engines turning over slowly till full pressure was restored. The leading stoker below the control platform was looking after the lubrication and extraction pumps which take the water out of the condenser and feed it to the boiler feed pumps, which in turn deliver it to the boiler rooms. He was up to his waist in water. It was still coming in. You could still see it rising. I was watching the bilge pump, the coupling for the electric motor, and I knew if it got above that it would put the electric motor out. That's why I opened the main inlet. I sucked out the floodwater, and told him to yell out when it got down to his knees, that we had it under control. I didn't bother to pump it dry because I had to think of the condenser—it needed water. Then we swiftly reversed the suction to take on the seawater again, so we had a bit of confidence then that we had it under control—and we could do it again if necessary.

We remained like that for some time until the first damage control was completed. The chief stoker then transferred fuel oil out of the damaged side of the ship and pumped it into the good side to bring her back up onto an even keel. We carried over 1700 tons of oil. In the meantime we were drawing away from the battle because we were helpless. All hands were lost in the switchboard room, and even though both the dynamo room and the gun control room were flooded, everybody got out of there.

As soon as we got the engines running we phoned to the bridge that we could proceed at slow speed, at about eight knots at that stage. Damage repair parties had restored communication by that time.

Did you have any idea at that time of what was going on up above?
No. I went on my normal watch below at six o'clock, 1800 hours, and before it ended action stations were sounded. I was there until three o'clock in the morning. During this time the cooks sent down sandwiches. At 0300 another chief came down to relieve me for a breather and I went up to the mess. I had a bottle of rum, about three tots, so I drank the lot. I downed that and it might as well have been water. It had no effect on me.

I was a bit tired. Mind you, it's surprising what energy you can find when there's danger around. I changed my overalls because they were wet through, as though I'd been swimming. I had a quick walk up on deck. We were out of sight of any action, and it was still dark. I went down again then and was down there until eight o'clock, when I could have a shower and breakfast and look for somewhere to sleep. Hammocks were not allowed during daylight hours. I had eight hours before my next watch.

We were steaming at about eight knots down towards Tulagi and arrived there just before sunset, just before they closed the submarine boom. We went in the harbour and out of sight of the open sea, around the corner, surrounded by jungle, and tied up—to a coconut tree at one end and a big telegraph-like post sticking out of the water at the other. We could see the seabed, it appeared about

Torpedo damage to Leander, *Calliope dock, Devonport, 1943.* Royal New Zealand Navy Museum, AAG 0019

a metre under the keel. Low tide! So that was that. By then we were pretty well on an even keel. The Yanks had an establishment ashore, so they came on board next morning at daybreak with a concrete mixer and builder's mix and various other things, and set that up on the upper deck. The stokers' mess deck—that's above the boiler room where this happened—had been blown up about a metre or two. It was all bent up. We didn't have the means of getting it down, but they covered it over in some way with timber and then poured concrete to cover the hole on the stokers' mess deck.

When did you become aware of the casualties?
When I went up for that hour, I went along the passageway. By then all the watertight doors were opened, so I went along the passageway by the boiler rooms and through the stokers' mess deck. I could smell human remains, burnt. Hot blood is a terrible smell. It had blown up from the boiler room into the stokers' mess deck. It was horrible. I learnt that the blast had blown up through the air intake. That's got a grating over it to stop people getting sucked down. The explosion blew back up. One of the four-inch guns was close, and it blew a lot of the crew overboard with the blast. They were lost. Some got caught in the guard rails; their mates pulled them back. They were injured. There were about 15 injured—some down in the stokers' mess deck and some off the gun deck. We learnt of these things next morning.

They were all killed in the boiler room, and the electricians in the main switchboard room. Some were buried there at Tulagi.

There were prayers for the dead, do you have any memory of that?

Yes, that would be in Tulagi after we got in. It would be that night or the next night, because in the daytime everybody would be flat out working on damage control. The Anglican padre conducted that, and everybody went, except those who had to be on watch in the harbour. The whole ship's company. I can't remember much of it, except that it was a very sad, sombre occasion.

Then we had to get down to it and work. There was nothing the OAs (ordnance artificers) could do, so they were given to me as a damage control team, helping with the repairs. They were not familiar with the engine or boiler rooms, so I had to show them what to do. We had a whole list of things and we had to tick it off, 'not complete' or 'complete', each day until we had made all possible temporary repairs.

It took 10 days working from half past seven in the morning until nine o'clock at night in the tropics, in hot weather.

Tell me about the ladder that you built.

We always practised action stations, even in peacetime. My action station was the forward dynamo room with 13 other people. We had to go through the stokers' mess deck, and through a watertight door, which strictly had to be kept shut until the all-clear. I thought, If the ship's damaged and this place leaks, we're going to be drowned. The ventilator shaft was at one end of the dynamo room, about a yard square, leading up to the four-inch gun deck, and it came out near the four-inch guns and behind the bridge. There was a big grating over it to stop people falling down. I thought, Well, that's the only way out. So I got the OK to build a steel ladder as an escape route. I drew the steel from the stores and made the ladder. I went up and took all the screws out holding the grating, and they were brass screws so that they wouldn't rust, quarter-inch brass screws. I cut them short with a hacksaw so there were only about two threads left, just enough to hold it in place, then I climbed up the ladder and put my back against the wall of the ventilator shaft and booted the grating and broke the screws and climbed out. Then I made a new set of very short screws, put it all back together. When the torpedo happened the people in this dynamo room were immediately swimming, because the wall between the switchboard room and the dynamo room was punctured enough to let the place be flooded. They were swimming in the dark, but they knew where to go, so they got up, went up the short ladder which ended at the watertight door, and then just stepped across and transferred to the new ladder. And got out. Nobody was hurt, nobody was drowned.

Did anyone acknowledge that you'd saved those lives?
One chap said, 'Thanks, Spud.'

And that was it?
Yes. It was a highlight for me, amongst all the dreary sadness. But it was just another part of the job.

In preparation for bringing **Leander** *back to New Zealand from Tulagi, the crew did a 'basin trial'.*

You tie it up to the wharf after you come out of dock, and get up steam and just turn the engines over slowly for a couple of hours or so. We did a basin trial tied up to our coconut tree for about four hours.

We had no fresh water, the Yanks supplied us with that. They sent aboard tanks of water to fill the two boilers. We filled them up to just under half a glass, because water expands when it heats. When it comes up to half a glass, that's what you steam at. We got the evaporators going to make our own fresh water, because we wanted seven tons in the engine room. We had two 30-ton tanks just forward of all the damage, but we didn't know whether they were contaminated or not so we didn't use them. We had a ready-

Placing a drum of ammunition in one of Leander's *small anti-aircraft guns.* ATL, War History Collection, DA-01884

use seven-ton tank in the engine room. So we filled that up, and all the fresh-water drinking tanks, and having done that then we could turn the engines over, so we 'lit up' in the normal way. We started up the various auxiliary machines such as lubrication pumps and extractor pumps, feed pumps and all that sort of thing, and then started the engines slowly turning. I think we did that for about four hours. We tested the water frequently, every half hour we got a test tube and drew off water. We had some nitrate of silver, in a little glass bottle with a spout on it and a lid on it that would only allow drops to come out, and we'd just drop two drops of that in the water and if it remained clear, that was good. We had good clean water of our own. If it showed a cloud just like cigarette smoke in the water, then we knew it had salt in it. Boiler water had to be completely pure. Better than drinking water!

Next day the second boiler was lit up, we had our own dynamos, we had our own fresh water, and so we set sail. The ship was on an even keel. It was a huge hole, you know, you could drive a bus through it.

We left Tulagi and were steaming for a couple of days at about economical speed, about 11 knots. We were escorted by a couple of American destroyers. There could have been a submarine attack and at 11 knots you were easy prey, so we decided to see what we could do with two boilers instead of six. We got up to 18 knots, which was pretty good—faster than a submarine, so we had a chance. We knew we could manoeuvre a bit if there was a submarine scare, because the Americans had submarine detection apparatus and radar—good radar, better than us. A couple of Zeros came over from somewhere but we fought those off. They had a go at us. I think the Yanks got one.

Leander *arrived back at the Devonport naval dock in Auckland.*

Volunteers got the bodies and remains out of the damaged part, and then there was the funeral. There were only two that could be recognised. We always wore an identity disc around our neck, a little bit of hard red plastic stuff with your name and blood group and official number on it. And religion, I think. To identify people. But they couldn't identify anything except two of them, just bits and pieces, body pieces. At the funeral they were buried in the one grave as the unknown sailor, but there are headstones and funeral plots for the other two now. My mate, the senior chief engine room artificer, was one. I had to take over his duties. Later his wife—they had one child, a little girl—was so overcome that she committed suicide with the child. She turned on the gas and put their heads in the gas oven at home.

Funeral for sailors killed when Leander *was torpedoed.* James Murphy collection

Twenty-eight [were killed] and 15 injured. While we were in Tulagi doing the repairs we were allowed to send a signal back to your mother or sister or brother or whatever, and it stated the name and address, so many words, four or five words and your name. So that was good.

Can you remember what you said?
'Safe and well love Jim.' That went by wireless, as we called it in those days. All accomplished just in one day. It came to my wife Nora as a telegram, delivered to the door.

> *Jim was then posted to minesweepers before going to HMNZS* Gambia *in mid-1945. He was in Australia when he heard about the atomic bombs that had been dropped on Hiroshima and Nagasaki. He then went to Japan and joined* Gambia. *They went ashore in both Tokyo and Yokohama.*

Could you see the effects of the war on those places?

Yes. They had been bombed or bombarded. Tokyo particularly was knocked about, but the Emperor's palace was intact. Beautiful grounds around it, and the water around it looked like a moat and had lots of goldfish in it and beautiful little bridges going over it to the palace.

He describes his feelings when he heard that the war was over.

A little relief. You were hyped up in a way, permanently, and then you just went flat. It's hard to describe the feeling. It felt different that you weren't tensed up, ready for anything to happen, any minute of

Soldiers sightseeing in Japan. ATL, War History Collection, J-0185

the day and night. That was all gone. And the excitement was over. And you just drooped. It sounds strange, doesn't it? Strange, too, to have the scuttles (portholes) open and deadlights (covers) folded back after six years!

In that ship we went down and helped get prisoners of war onto the hospital ships. That was just a bit south of Tokyo. We were anchored off the coast, and so was the hospital ship. Showers were provided ashore for showering and delousing and giving the soldiers or airmen or whoever clothes, and then taking them in the boats out to the hospital ships. I personally didn't have anything to do with it, because I was required aboard.

The men from **Gambia** *who helped ferry the POWs described their condition to the others aboard.*

They were in rags and were just like skeletons, walking skeletons. Very weak and crying and hanging on to each other. They said it was really pitiable and made them very angry to think that so-called human beings would treat other people like that. They were absolutely disgusted.

Did you ever consider that you could be taken prisoner?
Yes. You had several options. To be burnt alive, to be scalded, to be overboard and drown, to be overboard and eaten by the sharks, to die of dehydration if you were out there afloat—there were all sorts of options, survival being the preferred one! But there wasn't much use getting too upset about it, it didn't help.

Before you were attacked at Kolombangara, did you see a lot of Japanese ships and aircraft?
No, because we were mostly right out in the middle of the ocean. We were chasing and looking for Japanese ships and submarines. We met some sometimes. I remember one night we had a go, and we weren't hit, but we came into harbour and one American cruiser had her bows blown off and the deck had folded down like a door in the front. Another one had—I forget whether it was a torpedo or a bomb—stuck in the hull down near the stern, so she was in a very precarious situation. There were others with pretty severe damage but still floating.

Once up there, when in port, the Catholics on board went to Mass on an aircraft carrier. I think it

Tokyo Bay, 8 September 1945. Mt Fuji is in the background. James Murphy collection

was the *Enterprise*. We went aboard one Sunday morning and were invited down to the chief's mess to have coffee. They said, 'Will you have cream?' We didn't even have milk! And they had an ice-cream shop, and you'd see sailors going around with a lump of ice cream as big as your head in a container. They gave us a whole lot of New Zealand apples, the best apples I've ever tasted anywhere in New Zealand.

Did the American sailors' lot seem to be better than your lot?
Oh yes. Yes, oh yes, yes. From talking to them, it was more like hotel living. And the food was different, too. We might have sausages for breakfast. We used to call them sawdust sausages, because that's what

HMNZS Gambia. Royal New Zealand Navy Museum, AAI 0026

they tasted like, and then you might have McConachies herrings in tomato sauce for lunch, then you might have kippers for the evening meal. The next day they'd change it and you'd have kippers for breakfast.

At sea, every third night when my engine-room crew used to have the middle watch (midnight till four), some of the lads used to go around to the officers' supplies cages on deck somewhere, and somehow or other manage to cut chunks of meat off legs of beef. They'd get some vegetables, and we'd put it all in a billy and put it under a steam jet and make a stew. And they'd pinch spuds and onions, and we used to put them up on the turbines underneath the lagging, and we knew from the speed we were doing how long they would take to cook, because the higher the speed the higher the temperature of the engines. This was on the *Leander*. That was the best ever meal.

The potatoes used to be kept in a sort of a cage on the upper deck with a locked door, well aerated in sacks. But they used to go bad. They wouldn't last long in the tropics. They were so bad they couldn't be peeled, so they were just all tipped into a huge container and boiled up in the galley. Came out as a grey, semi-liquid mess.

The bread used to get cockroaches and weevils in it. You'd hold it up to the light, you could see the cockroaches because they were brown and you could pick them out, but with the weevils it was a bit harder because they were white. You'd finish up with a slice of bread that looked like wire netting.

> *After the war Jim found it difficult to find a job with a decent salary, but was eventually offered one requiring a merchant service certificate. Later he worked as a metalwork and engineering teacher. He and his wife Nora, who died in 1999, had three children. He reflects on his Pacific war service.*

We didn't mind scrapping in the Pacific; it was nearer home. It was a local thing, whereas before that it was a long way away from home.

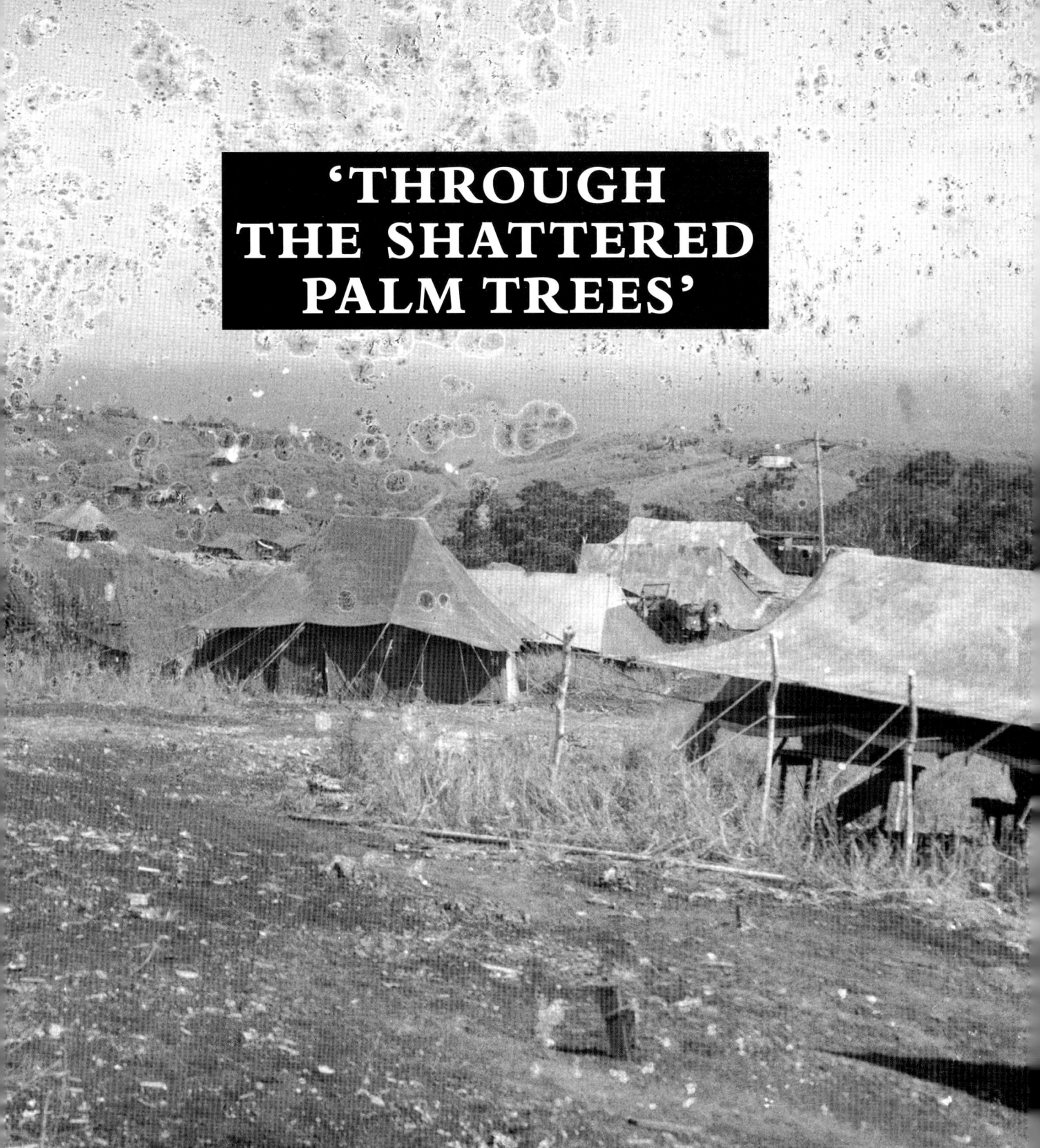

'THROUGH
THE SHATTERED
PALM TREES'

NOEL ROSOMAN, 545938,
DRIVER, 4 ARMY SERVICE CORPS

Noel Rosoman, the son of Elsie and William Rosoman, was born in 1913 in Feilding, where he attended Lytton Street School and Feilding Agricultural College before leaving to drive a baker's van. In 1939 he married Evelyn Foot. They had a young daughter by the time he was conscripted in August 1942. Noel trained at Trentham and arrived in New Caledonia on 31 December 1942.

THE SHIP THAT WE WERE supposed to have gone on was torpedoed up in the islands. That's why we waited for the USS *West Point*. It was built as the SS *America* to capture the Atlantic blue ribbon for the fastest crossing between New York and London. It was finished, apparently, just as the war broke out, and soon after that the army requisitioned it for a troop carrier. We slept in bunks, three high on 10 decks.

Mealtimes used to be a real circus. You can imagine 5000 men trying to get a meal. We used to walk around one deck, down the companionway, walk around the next, down and down and down till we got to the galley and got our meal. You picked up a stainless steel plate, it had six or seven indentations on it, and you walked past the row of the chaps and they'd splash a dollop of this and a dollop of something else on your plate as you walked by. After you had your meal you had to clean your plate in boiling water and put it back on a shelf. We had to eat our meal standing up. It was all tinned stuff, and they had a cunning arrangement on the back of the boat like a big roller, and they flattened all the tins so they'd sink—I suppose so they wouldn't give themselves away with a floating tin where a Jap submarine might see it. It was quite a massive thing, and they just poked all the tins in it and crunch, crunch, crunch, and they dropped over the stern. So the Pacific rim is probably lined with tins.

Previous page: *New Zealand camp at Guadalcanal, probably 1943.* ATL, War History Collection, WH-0158
Above: *Noel Rosoman, August 1942.* Noel Rosoman collection

Noel and Evelyn Rosoman (centre) on their wedding day, 24 June 1939.
Noel Rosoman collection

There was a constant cacophony of orders coming over the loudspeakers for the crew. 'Now hear this.' Everything was 'Now hear this', and we had to do this and do that. When it came to mealtimes, what came over was, 'Now hear this, all New Zealand troops lay below to the galley for chow.'

I had heard of the blue Pacific Ocean, but I didn't realise how blue it was. It was a very, very deep blue colour, much darker than I thought it would be. There were also flying fish. They'd zip up out of the water and spread their long pectoral fins just like the wings of a plane. They seemed to have a little rudder under their tail, and they'd wriggle that and scoot along the top of the water for about 12 or 15 metres and flop back into the water. Six or eight would fly out at a time.

That was my first overseas trip. I'd never been outside of New Zealand prior to that. I was fortunate being in the Army Service Corps, because we were always behind the fighting men. Our job was to keep them supplied with ammunition, petrol, and rations.

What was your first sight of New Caledonia, can you remember?
Yes. It's a long rocky island. There's a reef around it and the entrance through the reef was about

Soldiers playing cards aboard a transport in the Pacific. ATL, War History Collection, F-44789-1/2

10 kilometres from Noumea wharf. They had a submarine barrage there. A little tug picked it up and waited until we'd gone through, then they brought the submarine barrage thing back again.

The whole of the American 7 Fleet was in Noumea harbour. There were little bays all the way along, and all these big battleships were anchored in the smaller bays. There must have been 10 or a dozen or more huge battleships.

New Caledonia lies roughly the same as New Zealand, roughly north and south. The east coast is the same as our east coast—dry—and the west coast must get more rain because there's quite a bit of small bush on that. On the east coast there were stunted niaouli gum trees, grey in colour. It was a rather dismal-looking landscape.

We arrived early in the morning. All the young chaps said, 'Ooh la la! We'll be able to see the French mademoiselles', but they were disappointed because we sat there till just on midday and then a Dutch cargo ship pulled up alongside. The 4 ASC transferred to this boat, and we sailed all the afternoon until it was getting just on dark and we arrived at Nepoui, three-quarters of the way up New Caledonia.

It was a desolate place. It was nothing. There was a long skinny wharf and that was all. We had to turn into wharfies straight away, and for 24 hours—three eight-hour shifts—we unloaded American Liberty ships with all the rations. There was just enough room to back your truck along, and then they would bring the rations up in a sling out of the hold and dump it on your truck. You'd have to stack it up and when you got a full load you took off, and there was a line of trucks waiting to back onto the wharf.

We were camped at Nepoui itself. It was just an open countryside. There were niaouli trees. We were a bit fortunate because 14 Brigade had gone through the same procedure a month earlier. They were already there, and they had a hot meal waiting for us.

Noel spent his time driving trucks carrying petrol and other supplies between Nepoui and Noumea.

We had what they call the LAD, light aid detachment, and they maintained vehicles, changed the oil and did that sort of thing. We had a kiwi on the front doors. It greatly fascinated the Americans. Different ones said, 'What's that goddam chick on the side of your truck?' Another one said, 'Oh, it's K 1 W 1.' Another bloke said, 'It's a Kywy.' 'Kiwi' was written underneath. The trucks were all grey with a black kiwi on them. One chap had a pair of deer antlers on the front of his truck; another called his 'Misscarriage'.

Noel Rosoman (left) at Bouloupari, New Caledonia, 1943.
Noel Rosoman collection

He exchanged letters regularly with his wife.

They usually delivered the mail on our morning parade. Any letters, they'd call you out and you'd have to go out and get them. Our daughter by then was three, and on the bottom I used to draw three or four little palm trees for her.

We needed long sleeves for the mosquitoes. At five o'clock you had to put your shirt on and roll them down. There was no risk during the day. They only flew at night, fortunately.

We had a beer issue every Thursday afternoon. Two one-litre bottles of beer, and the officers got their choice of a bottle of spirits of some sort. I was not interested in drinking warm beer, and there was always a flock of Americans once they knew the day of our beer issue. They'd always arrive in the afternoon, and I sold all my beer for $2 a bottle. And they made the offer that if you could nick a bottle of spirits they'd give you $45 for it.

Did many of the blokes sell their beer?
Oh yes, quite a lot. I'm not a beer drinker to be perfectly honest, and warm beer was even worse. I used to play poker in Feilding in the Working Men's Club before I was married, and so on New Caledonia there was about five of us had a school. At night-time there was nothing to do in New Caledonia. We used to be notified when there was a movie on in the American camp, and we used to go and watch the

Kiwi troops read mail from home, Vella Lavella. ATL, War History Collection, WH-0217

new movies from the States. We sat out in the paddock on the grass. If it rained too hard they called it a day and you had to go home.

What were the Americans like?

By and large, they were very good. They were very interested in us, our strange accent, and we got on very well with them. They were no bother at all.

In September 1943, Noel left New Caledonia for Guadalcanal in the Solomon Islands.

It was very early in the morning. The three ships stood offshore and they unloaded them with small assault boats. They rushed ashore and dropped the flap at the front. They had eight of them to each of the cargo ships, and it took us seven hours to unload 90 days' rations for 5000 men.

Then we went through the shattered palm trees. They were all shot off because the American Marines landed on the same beach and, before they landed, their battleships blew the hell out of the area with their heavy guns. You'd swear that they'd been along and cut them off level about 10 or 12 feet high, all the coconut palms growing along the shore. We chained the boxes of rations off the beach through the shattered palms and onto a big open area. We of the Army Service Corps were responsible for the rations and were directing the chaps to put all the different rations in different heaps. After we'd unloaded the ships, it took us a week to shift all the rations from the beach to the ration dump at our camp.

By this stage the Japanese troops were further north.

14 Brigade landed on Vella Lavella. The Americans had Vella Lavella half-cleared of Japanese, and so they retired and our battalions took over and cleared the Japanese from the north of Vella Lavella.

What were your impressions of Guadalcanal?

There were flocks of shrieking sulphur-crested Australian white cockatoos, and they drove you to distraction. They never stopped shrieking all day. The only other birdlife I saw were brown jungle hens, about the size of a pukeko. At night you could hear these jungle hens scattering around. They gave you the creeps a bit—it might have been a Jap.

In October 1943, Noel's unit moved up to Mono, in the Treasury Islands between Vella Lavella and Bougainville, on which New Zealand and American troops had landed to clear it of Japanese.

I was in the second wave. I was a bit lucky. I missed the landing, and it was five days before the second wave arrived on Mono Island. When they landed on the beach there was a pillbox, and there were 13 Japanese in it. On the landing ship tanks, right in the front, was a big RD-8 bulldozer with a big blade. They needed that to make a track for the trucks to get ashore. I wasn't there, the chaps told me that there was a mountain gun up on a rise. The Japanese were firing at them and they were heaving hand grenades, and on two occasions when the firing from this hillside got too intense, the LSTs pulled out. Eventually the bulldozer driver got off and got on top of this pillbox, and I'm afraid he killed the whole 13 Japs. He came from the back because they didn't have any fire holes at the back. All the fire holes were to the front, to the sea, so they couldn't shoot at him. He had his blade up to protect himself and squashed them, unfortunately. He was decorated for bravery later on.

Then when the battalion and the troops arrived, they upped the hill and captured the mountain gun which kept firing at them, and the ones that were throwing the grenades took off, apparently. It took 12 days for the troops to make Mono Island secure. I think it was 245 Japs they killed, and took eight prisoners.

Were the ASC men going on shore on that first landing?
Yes. Because we had rations and ammunition. Mostly ammunition, because that's what the battalions needed. I landed five days later.

What was your first impression of Mono Island?
It was small and very hilly. It was only about 12 kilometres across. The reason the Americans wanted the Treasury group was they were getting up in the Pacific and they needed airstrips. We had 25 American surveyors attached to our unit and they surveyed, and chopped the jungle down. They made a fighter strip, and the planes used to use that and get a refill of petrol if needed.

We had the ration dump, and we sorted out the incoming rations and made out the 10-day ration break, gave it out to the troops, and that was about it. Nothing else you could do. It was only a small island.

Charging off an LCI onto a Mono Island beach under fire. ATL, War History Collection, F-44798-1/2

Did you get bored?

Not really. We were far too busy. We had two or three air raids the first couple of nights. There were 22,000 Japs, they reckoned, still on Bougainville, and the original lot sat there for seven and a half days hoping that the Japs didn't come down and wipe them out. We had an American four-gun 90-millimetre unit quite close to us, and when these raids came over they fired their guns off and our tent would go whoof! We got the muzzle blast from the guns. There was only one day-raid and the pilot got shot down for his trouble. He was a fighter-bomber and he dropped a stick of bombs in Blanche harbour, but by then they had the airstrip going and American planes went up and shot him down.

How long did it take you to get used to the heat?

I suppose you would never really get used to it. On Stirling Island we were right in the jungle, and it was very sticky and hot, but you just had to put up with it. There were a lot of pretty butterflies, but at night, if you held or hung a lighted torch outside your tent, there were a whole lot of very pretty moths. They had coloured wings and fancy scalloped wings. There were also fireflies with a winking fluorescent green light.

Noel was able to attend a concert at a mission station while on Mono Island.

There were about 12 island boys who sang for us. There were Methodist missions right throughout the Solomon Islands. The missionaries not only preached the gospel but they also looked after them. They used to have gardens and grow their own vegetables. So these chaps sang several songs. There was a seven-year-old lad and he had an amazingly high soprano voice, a true voice, and after they'd finished he came over to me and pointed up to the sky and said, 'Jesus is up there.' I said, 'Yes, that's right.' So he'd absorbed some of the gospel.

After about two months on Mono I got tropical sores. They came out in a big blister, and when the blister burst you had a running sore. I had half a dozen on each leg. When I reported sick to the RAP (the Regimental Aid Post), the doctor put ointment on them and wrapped them up. That wasn't a very good thing to do because they got steadily worse, and after about a week I reported to have the dressing done again and he said, 'They're not going to heal here, so I'm going to send you back to Guadalcanal.' So I said three hearty cheers. I was fair and ginger-headed, thin-skinned, and I wasn't made for the tropics, I'm afraid.

I went back on an LST and I had to report to the doctor. He said, 'These 90-millimetre shell cases'—they were a big shell case you could get your foot in—'your treatment is you will stand a leg in each of these shell cases with Condy's crystals and warm water.'

So I did that morning and night, and in the two and a half days it took us to get back to Guadalcanal they were starting to heal. He told me after dunking my legs to roll my pants up and stand on the deck in the shade to get the breeze.

I had about a week in hospital, and that's when an American Negro came down about the first night I was there, and he was very chuffed that we'd talk to him because I'm afraid the American troops there looked down on them. He was so delighted to think that we'd talk to him that he used to come down every night after that and bring us candy bars. I think the Americans shunned them, from what I could see. You could see they never mixed with them.

In hospital, two American sailors used to talk to us. They used to play a card game called pinochle. When they were discharged after two or three days one of them turned to his mate and said, 'When we get back to our ship I'll be able to say to my buddies, "Come on all you bloody jokers. Come and get a bloody cup of tea."' He picked up the New Zealand language all right.

A surgical station on Guadalcanal. ATL, War History Collection, F–41591–1/2

Did you pick up any Americanisms?

Yes, but I couldn't repeat them. They had some very foul language.

When I came out of the hospital I wasn't doing anything much. I was attached to a unit. I think I must have got a slight touch of dengue fever. I felt very off, had a bad head for a few days. One morning the sergeant came round. He said, 'I want six volunteers.' Of course, in the army you volunteer for nothing. So no volunteers. The next morning he came around, 'I still want six volunteers.' I was improving by then and I said, 'I'll be one.' Eventually there were five others, and it happened they had room for six chaps to go back to New Caledonia. I was in what they called an APR camp: awaiting passage return.

There were a number of us there and we did eventually get on this boat, the *Talamanca*. It was the middle of winter and it was a very rough sea. I was seasick for two and a half days and had nothing to eat.

Evelyn Rosoman with her two-year-old daughter Noeline. Noel Rosoman collection

Noel returned to New Zealand aboard the **Talamanca** *in June 1944.*

Probably there were several hundred on the boat. We were welcomed by a member of parliament and all the ladies in the shed. We had a drink and something to eat, and they put us on a train and we took off back to our respective destinations.

When you came back and got home, what was it like seeing your little girl again?

It was very good. She was rather mystified about me for a while. We met on the Aramoho station at Wanganui. My wife and Noeline, my daughter, were waiting, the only ones on the platform. I was very relieved. And Noeline said, 'Do you love me?', and I said yes. Just under two years I was away, altogether.

I was manpowered to the firm of Walpole & Paterson, a big firm of builders. After about six months I was called up again, and had to go through a medical and passed that again. I was given a one-way ticket to Trentham. It was 1945 by then and the war in Europe had finished. They wanted to bring home the New Zealand troops from Italy, but they had to garrison Italy for 12 or 18 months after the war and they wanted reinforcements. I was to be one of those. When I got this call-up my wife was due to have our second child, so I applied for three months' extension, which they granted, and then I got a second one-way ticket to Trentham. By that time my wife was in the hospital having the child. So I appealed again and the chap in charge of the appeal board said, 'After your wife has had the child you will be quite happy to go back overseas?' I said yes. They gave me a month or so, then I got a third one-way ticket to Trentham. I had no more excuses, so I gave notice to the firm of builders I was driving for and I went to the Drill Hall just before lunchtime and got my uniform. I took it home to the flat we were living in and when I tried an anklet on, I broke one of the straps on it. I went back at one o'clock and said to the chap, 'Will you change this pair of anklets for me?', and he looked at me and said, 'You were here just before dinner, weren't you, and you told me your wife had two children?' I said yes. He said, 'Well, as a matter of fact, at one o'clock when I got back from lunch I got a ring from Wellington, and they're not going to take any more married men with two children.' So I stalled them off right to the minute. The next day I had to go back and get my job back driving the truck for the firm of builders.

And that was the end of the war for you?
That was the end of it.

> *In recent years Noel has attended Anzac Day dawn parades.*

I quite enjoyed the last two, getting out there at five o'clock, the plane flying over, the four soldiers standing on each corner of the cenotaph firing three rounds each. Frightened the hell out of everybody.

And what do you think about when they play the Last Post?
I always feel sorry for those who didn't come back, because there was a lot of them who got lost at sea, shot down. There were all the soldiers in the Bourail cemetery in New Caledonia. I feel a bit sad for them.

> *Noel continued working as a driver for Walpole & Paterson for 32 years. He and his wife still live*
> *in Wanganui. He reflects on his war service.*

I went and came back. You had no option. You just had to get on with the job and do what you had to do. We were branded as coconut bombers, as distinct from the men of steel in the desert. We were either coconut bombers or banana pickers. But that soon dropped. That didn't take any skin off my nose. It didn't worry me.

'SMOKE AND FLAMES
FROM BURNING
AIRCRAFT'

JOHN McKAY, NZ7378,
ABLE SEAMAN, ROYAL NAVY

John McKay was born in Auckland in 1922, the son of Margaret and Robert McKay, who was a ship's engineer. He worked for the Public Trust Office after leaving Auckland Grammar School, and volunteered for the Territorial Force in 1940. After three years there he joined the navy, in part to follow in his father's footsteps. He trained on HMNZS Tamaki *on Motuihe Island in the Hauraki Gulf.*

WE HAD HUGE KITBAGS full of clothing, et cetera, and to get to the base from the wharf at Motuihe had to go up quite a steep road. We walked up with a hammock which used to roll up like a sausage over one shoulder, the kitbag over the other shoulder. We thought, My God, what are we letting ourselves in for? We had very, very intensive training. Marching and drill and seamanship and tying knots and all the rest of it. Keeping the ship clean, scrubbing, learning to be a lookout. We had a bit of radar training just to show us how radar worked.

John joined the Royal Navy after his training on Tamaki.

We were told we were going on final leave. I had to go home and tell my mother. We reported back to *Philomel*. We were there for a day or two and then we were given tickets for the train down to Wellington. One night in some barracks in Wellington. I was quite excited, as you could imagine.

John left New Zealand on HMS Ranee *and arrived in Colombo, Ceylon (Sri Lanka), at the end of February 1944. There he joined HMS* Illustrious, *an aircraft carrier in the British Eastern Fleet. While on watch, John was a lookout on the bridge.*

Previous page: *HMNZS Tamaki, Motuihe Island.* Royal New Zealand Navy Museum, ABZ-0095
Above: *John McKay, 1943.* John McKay collection

Above: *HMS* Illustrious. Royal New Zealand Navy
Museum, ACJ 0979

Right: *John McKay (left) and his friend Arthur Ruff in
Sydney. John had just had his white uniform made in
Ceylon (Sri Lanka)*. John McKay collection

We had radar, but radar would pick planes or ships up long-distance. When they came close there was nothing like the human eye.

What did you do if you saw something?
You had a thing around your neck that you spoke into, and you'd report to whoever you were supposed to report to. It wasn't radio, it was all wire. It was a primitive type of a thing, but it did the job.

Apart from watches, what were your duties on the ship?
Keeping the ship clean. There was a lot scrubbing of decks, especially the bridge and the superstructure, where it was all a type of lino on the decks. They had to be scrubbed spotless—on our hands and knees.

I wasn't a gunner, but we had to help keep the guns and gun platforms clean. We had to make sure that ammunition was readily available, and at action stations very often if there were any men to spare you got into the ammunition train, which was to bring the ammunition from the magazines up into the gun turrets. The magazines were low down, right near the bottom of the ship, and they'd go in various carriers right up to the gun turrets. Machinery took it up, ammunition lifts.

> He recalls what happened when the ship went to action stations.

On an aircraft carrier when planes were flying off to go on an operation, action stations would be called for dawn, because the planes would always go off at dawn. So the whole ship would go to action stations. Everybody, no matter if you'd been on watch or what you were doing, you'd all go to action stations. The bugle would blow over the public address system: Hands to action stations. Everyone knew what that meant. It meant that you dropped what you were doing and it would be a matter of going like hell to where you were supposed to be. If in the course of the day the ship was under, or was about to be under, attack by planes, action stations would sound and you'd have to get there in a hurry. The radar would locate the incoming enemy planes—which were known as bandits—40 or 50 miles away,

Anti-flash gear is worn by men placing shells in the hydraulic hoist of an Australian cruiser. Australian War Memorial, Neg. 304897

I suppose, so you'd have time to get to action stations, the gunners to their guns and the lookouts to their lookout places. In the meantime, by the use of radar, the fighter direction room would direct our fighters out to meet these incoming bandits. If you happened to have a radar screen handy you could see the two echoes on the radar screen, and hopefully they'd join up. Our fighter planes would usually shoot most of them down.

Where did you go on action stations?
Up onto the top, to the air defence position. That's where the air defence officers were stationed. They would give directions to the guns. When action stations finished you'd get the pipe: Hands to cruising stations. 'Cruising stations' was just normal watch.

We all wore anti-flash gear. Normally at sea we just wore shorts and nothing else, but at action stations we had to wear clean overalls because of any wounds. Clean overalls and anti-flash gloves, big,

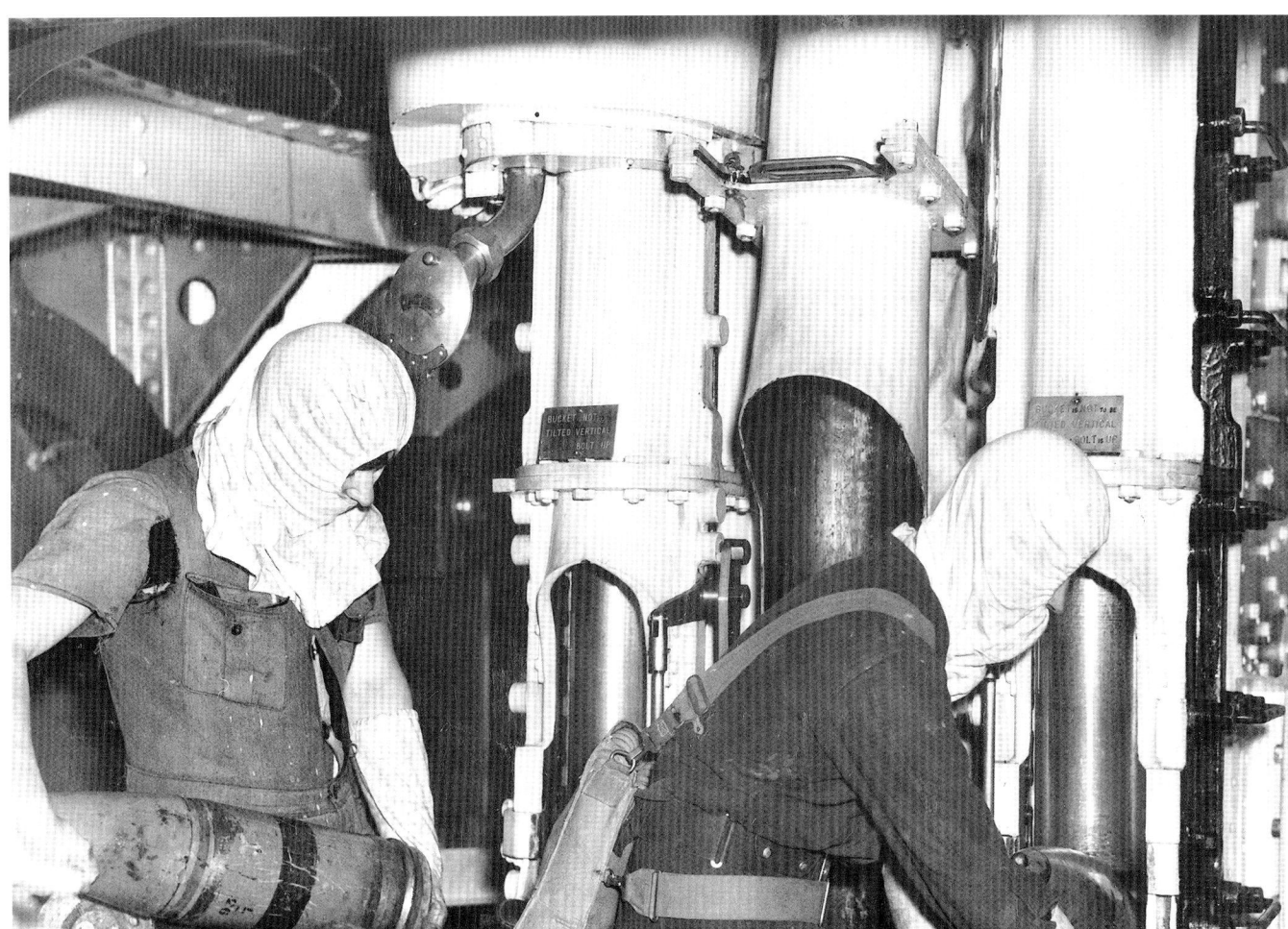

white asbestos gloves and a big white hood which you can just see through, pulled right down over your neck. It was called anti-flash gear against flash from guns. We had to have our lifebelts with us so we could put them on.

Tell me about your issue of rum each day.

It was mixed with water in the proportion of two to one. Two water, one rum. It was the equal of a railway cup full of rum and water. Quite a substantial tot, it was.

It was quite a ritual. About 11.30 over the address system would be the pipe: Up spirits. And then with one voice all those on the deck would shout out, 'Stand fast the Holy Ghost.' 'Holy Ghost' being the spirit, of course. 'Stand fast' was the naval expression for 'accept'. So then it was the job of—you took it in turns—two men who were termed 'rum bosuns' to go to the central position in the ship where the

Rum issue. This is on board HMS Leander. Royal New Zealand Navy Museum, AAG 0378

rum was brought up from the rum locker way down below and was very, very carefully mixed, tipped into a great big barrel. It was a beautiful varnished container with 'The King, God Bless Him' written in brass letters across it. The rum was tipped in, the water was tipped in. You took your receptacle up and it was measured out to the last drop. Then you took that receptacle full of rum back to the mess deck where all the cups, say 20, were put out. It was your job to measure it, with all eyes on you, with proper measuring things. Same amount, and there might be a little bit left. You'd always hang back, hoping that your mate would say, 'You have that.' They were brimming cups.

It was done at lunchtime, dinner time, when everybody except the men on watch would be there. You'd have yours, and that of the men on watches would all be put to one side so that when they came down theirs would be there.

Then another ritual went on. Invariably many members of the mess would owe other members of the mess certain amounts of their rum for having done various favours for them, such as doing their washing or cleaning their dinner plates. So the ritual then would be: 'Come on. You owe me sippers.' Or somebody might owe somebody gulpers, which was a bit more, and you might even go to half a tot. If you'd been wanting a job done very, very badly you might offer half a tot. That was half the cup. The ultimate, very seldom. The ultimate was the full tot.

John recalls watching the aircraft take off from the ship.

A lot of them would be arranged on the deck. The first half dozen or so fighters were sent off with the catapult, or the accelerator as it was called. They'd hook them up onto the thing. It was like a long railway line. The pilot would rev his engine up to take-off speed, and then on the signal the catapult would take off and boost the plane up into the air. The next one would be put on, and off it would go. It was to get rid of the front ones, which wouldn't have enough flying area to take off normally. When they got those out of the road the other planes would take off. Fighters first, being lighter. Last of all would be the torpedo bombers. They were heavy, so they were the last to take off. Some did go into the sea. We'd carry on, but a destroyer would pick them up.

It was the practice of anybody who was able to, to watch the planes landing back. Stretched across the flight deck were arrestor wires, about six, and as the planes came in their hooks came down. The object was for the hook to catch one of these wires. If it didn't catch the first one it would catch the

Men watch a Sea Fire land on HMS Indefatigable. Royal New Zealand Navy Museum, ACJ 0776

second, or the third or the fourth. The wires were heavily spring-loaded and stopped them.

If they missed those, the crash barriers were there. These were big steel wire barriers and they crashed into those, bang! If they crashed into the barriers, generally it destroyed the propeller and half the front of the plane, but the pilots would be all right. I witnessed this chap coming in. He'd been shot up and was very wobbly. He missed all the arrestor wires, crashed into the crash barrier, the plane went up on its nose and caught fire. Men with asbestos suits ran out to rescue the pilot. He got out and jumped onto the wing engulfed in flames and managed to run away, but he died. That's the only fatality I saw, but there were many, many crashes.

In January 1945 **Illustrious** *took part in an attack on oil installations at Palembang, on the island of Sumatra in what is now Indonesia.*

She steamed in at high speed. Our mess deck was right up forward and you could hear the seas crashing against the bows. Normally you didn't, but she was steaming in so fast that you could hear the seas crashing against the bows.

We were all a bit nervous, because we were told that it was a strongly defended area. Morning came. Action stations, and the planes took off. Away they went, and we retired a wee bit. After quite a long time, because the fighters were carrying extra petrol tanks, most of the planes came back. Quite a few were lost.

We thought, That's good, we've finished, but no, we were to have another go. It wasn't completely destroyed. In they went again the next day and pretty well destroyed the whole thing, but in the course of that action others were lost. They came back, landed, and we took off at high speed because Japanese planes came after us. None reached us. Any that came after us were shot down by our fighters.

It was announced later on: the following pilots had not returned. Read out names. I suppose they wanted the whole ship's company to know. It was awful. They did make a very good effort to pick up pilots who'd been shot down into the sea. We had a Walrus amphibian plane. If airmen were shot down, these planes could land, pick them up, come back and land on us. I can't remember whether they ever did that, but I do know that they had submarines off the coast and one or two pilots were picked up by our submarines. One of the very sad parts was that one or two who had been shot down and captured were beheaded later on.

Illustrious *was shelled during the action at Palembang.*

Twelve were killed, I think. We were being attacked. I was there, but I didn't see the planes attacking us. They came very close, close enough I believe to machine-gun the flight deck. The crew on an anti-aircraft cruiser, against all orders, were firing its big guns at the planes which were attacking our ship. Their guns were depressed far too low and instead of hitting planes the shells hit us, killed a pilot who had just landed, and another smashed into the side of the island, the bridge superstructure, and killed others there. There was a big stink about that.

Did you hear them hitting?

Yes, there was a hell of a bang. We thought they were bombs. It wasn't until things quietened down that we discovered that they were shells from the *Euryalus*. The dead were buried at sea, and the wounded were put ashore at Perth on our way down there.

Palembang was a very successful operation from the point of view of damage done. It destroyed the refinery, put it right out of action, but from the point of view of casualties, we had quite a few.

Illustrious *then joined the Pacific Fleet, which had bases at Manus Island in the Bismarck Archipelago and Leyte Gulf in the Philippines.*

We knew that the attack on Okinawa was coming up but the support fleet was to assemble at Ulithi [in the Caroline Islands], a coral atoll big enough to take the whole American and British fleets. It was an amazing sight. There were four of our carriers and there must have been a dozen American carriers, battleships, you name them. One day we all took off. That's when the American Marines and the army landed on Okinawa. The navy supported them with bombings, attacking airfields, that sort of thing.

The invasion of Okinawa began on 1 April 1945.

It was there that the kamikazes started. They attacked the Americans before they started on us, so we knew what to expect. We'd heard that they'd attacked the Americans and were sinking American carriers. We had some confidence, in that the American carriers had Oregon pine wooden flight decks and the kamikazes carried a 500-pound bomb as well as the plane full of petrol, so they'd go right through them, and set them on fire. But we had three or four inches of armoured steel on our flight decks and we thought we'd got some pretty good protection. And we did.

We were all dead scared of these kamikazes. That's what was worrying us. Especially as we'd heard what they were doing to the American carriers—they were sinking the carriers.

After operations at Okinawa we retired to Leyte, and while in Leyte in comes the *Formidable*. Over the PA system came a pipe: 'Would Able Seamen McKay and Ruff report to the Master-at-Arms' Office.' The two New Zealanders. We reported and were told, 'You fellows pack your gear, you're going to *Formidable*.' Dreadful. So we packed our swags, said a quick goodbye to everybody that we'd been with for so long, and off we went to *Formidable*. We were very sad about it. I got mad and annoyed about it.

A Japanese kamikaze aircraft, aflame from defensive gunfire, narrowly misses a US aircraft carrier in the Philippines. Australian War Memorial, Neg. 302728

They were transferred on 29 April 1945.

How different was it as a ship?

Physically she was a sister ship, but the atmosphere was completely different. There wasn't the same sort of willingness to do things. On *Illustrious*, if we were asked to do something we'd jump to it, but *Formidable* was quite different. It came down from the captain. I didn't like him. The men, the ratings, were good. We wondered what the hell we were doing there. I wasn't on the *Formidable* long enough to get to know anyone.

We started attacking the smaller islands south of Okinawa where there were airfields. That was our main job, putting airfields out of action to stop the Japanese air force playing too big a part in Okinawa.

John recalls when **Formidable** *was attacked by a kamikaze plane on 4 May 1945.*

They were picked up on the radar and our fighters went out to intercept them. They shot some down, but there were too many of them so quite a few of them got to the fleet. They were flying fairly high. Our big guns fired at them but they avoided those pretty well. They were right over the fleet, which meant that our fighter pilots were told not to attack directly. They came in closer and attacked other ships in the fleet, but this particular one came very close. I could see it, and it flew down the side of the ship. All the short-range guns opened up on it but didn't seem to have much effect. It still kept going. It flew right astern of the ship, and we thought he'd gone. But he hadn't. He flew astern of the ship and then circled around and chased the ship from the stern, of course flying much faster than we were going. He very rapidly caught up with the ship, came over the stern and then flew again alongside us. All of a sudden he flipped up on his back and crashed down onto the flight deck. He didn't dive from a great height. He flew along and then when he came abreast of the bridge he sort of flipped over and dived. Right into the deck. The bomb exploded, and the plane exploded too.

I didn't see the impact because I ducked. Quite a few chaps were killed and I got a bit of shrapnel in my arm. I thought, This is not too good, I'll have to try and get to the temporary sickbay. The officers' wardroom was the sickbay. This was still in the daytime and the ship was still at action stations. There was banging and crashing going on. We were pretty safe with this big steel flight deck.

HMS Formidable *arrives in Sydney harbour. The funnel was blackened when the kamikaze aircraft crashed on the deck.*
Australian War Memorial, Neg. P00444-047

I suppose there'd be 10 or 15 of us in the sickbay. As things quietened down in the evening the officers came in for their gin and tonics. And some offered us some, too. So we didn't refuse. We felt ourselves sorts of heroes, us poor ratings lying down in the wardroom.

Can you tell me what you thought when you saw the plane coming?
You thought it was going to crash on the flight deck. It's going to get a lot of us. Well, it did get a lot of us. On the flight deck level when I walked down there, you could see them lying there, obviously dead. That level seemed to get most of the blast. It penetrated there and killed quite a few of those chaps. That's where most of the deaths were, I think, in that area. There were none up where I was.

In a way you thought it's not going to crash, it's going to go past again, but then it flipped on the deck. He was a pretty shrewd customer; he didn't just dive and perhaps miss, he made sure of it. We thought he was going to machine-gun us.

There was a fairly big line-up of aircraft on the deck waiting to take off. So that would have meant that there would be a lot of flight deck men around. I should say some of those guys would have been the fellows that were burnt. The planes were damaged and they were burning, the planes on our flight deck. Quite nasty. The ship was on fire too, which didn't help, but they soon put that out. There was a smallish hole blown in the flight deck, which really was remarkable and a testament to the strength of the deck. They soon had that fixed up. They put beams across it and quick-drying cement. The planes were landing back on it again in two or three hours.

Before you went down to the sickbay, you could see the deck?
Yes. It was a real shambles. Well, it appeared to be. It wasn't really. It was all done very efficiently. Smoke and the flames from the burning aircraft, flight deck men here, there and everywhere trying to get rid of some over the side. They tried to use the cranes on each side of the ship, they were dumping planes off with those. Huge clouds of smoke coming from all over the place. It was a pretty grim scene, pretty quiet. Steam blowing out of the steam release valve. When the ship shut down speed, there was a huge accumulation of steam, normally in the boilers; it had to be blown out and it made quite a noise.

Can you remember what your thoughts were?
I wasn't really frightened. I was more frightened before it was to happen. After it had happened I think most people seemed fairly calm. I felt all right. Just as a matter of interest, she was struck by another one after I'd left her. Didn't cause as many casualties on that occasion.

We were in the wardroom overnight. The next day we were told we were going to be evacuated to the hospital ship *Maunganui*, a New Zealand hospital ship. We weren't much good left on the ship. We were transferred off the *Formidable* onto a destroyer. We went across in things like great big bread baskets. You were suspended as you went across and onto the destroyer, where the chaps grabbed hold of you. From the destroyer we were taken to another escort carrier. We'd got back to Leyte by this time. From the escort carrier we were admitted on board the *Maunganui*. She happened to be a New Zealand hospital ship, which was good. New Zealand crew, New Zealand nurses. It was marvellous. We were put into bed there, lovely bunks, white sheets. I wasn't in any pain. I was good. We had a wonderful time on her, concerts at night. From there we sailed down to Manus. We went ashore to the Manus airport to an American plane, a Dakota. Took off, landed in Milne Bay in New Guinea where we had to stop and refuel, and from there we went down to Townsville. It was getting cooler all the time, and we were just in shorts from the tropics. We stayed overnight in Townsville, and then the next day went down to Sydney and we were admitted to the Royal Naval Hospital.

Did you have any after-effects from your wounds?

I became completely deaf for about a week, I suppose, after the kamikaze. I gradually got most of my hearing back, but I still can't hear properly. I have a war pension for my hearing.

> *John returned to New Zealand and went back to the Public Trust Office until 1949, when he trained to be a teacher. He married his wife Joyce in 1946, and the couple have three daughters. John retired from teaching as headmaster of Hora Hora School in Whangarei. He reflects on his war experiences.*

It's a good thing over and done with, I know that. I'm anti-war now. I say that quite clearly. War seems to break out for any reason now, whereas that one was a good reason for stopping Hitler and Tojo and co. At the present time I can't see any real justification. Those are my sentiments.

I found the discipline in the Royal Navy was good. It wasn't harsh, not in my experience, not on *Illustrious* at any rate. It was not easy-going, but it was friendly, the officers were professional, they knew what they were doing, they were good seamen, and I think they taught us to be pretty good sailors or seamen.

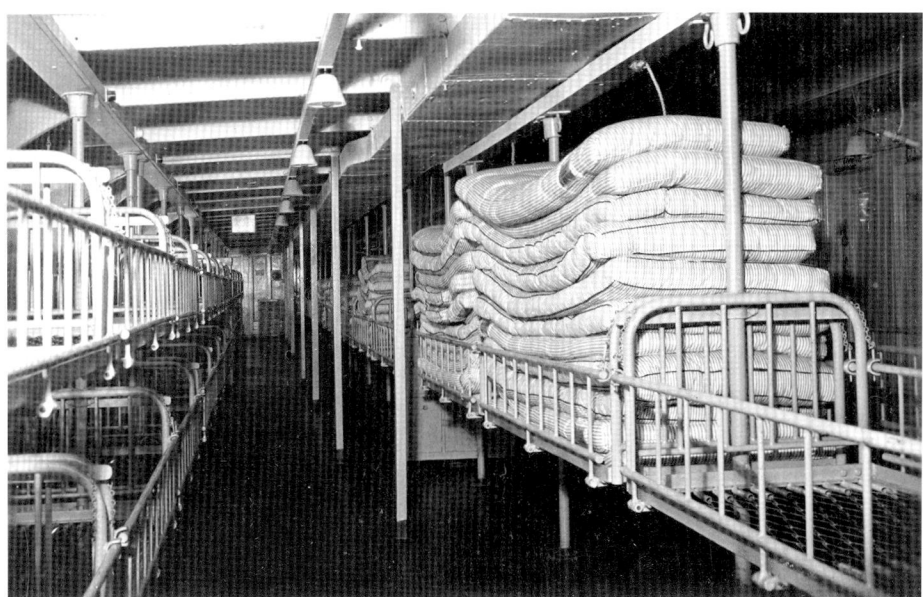

A ward on HMNZHS Maunganui. ATL, War History Collection, F-3083-1/2

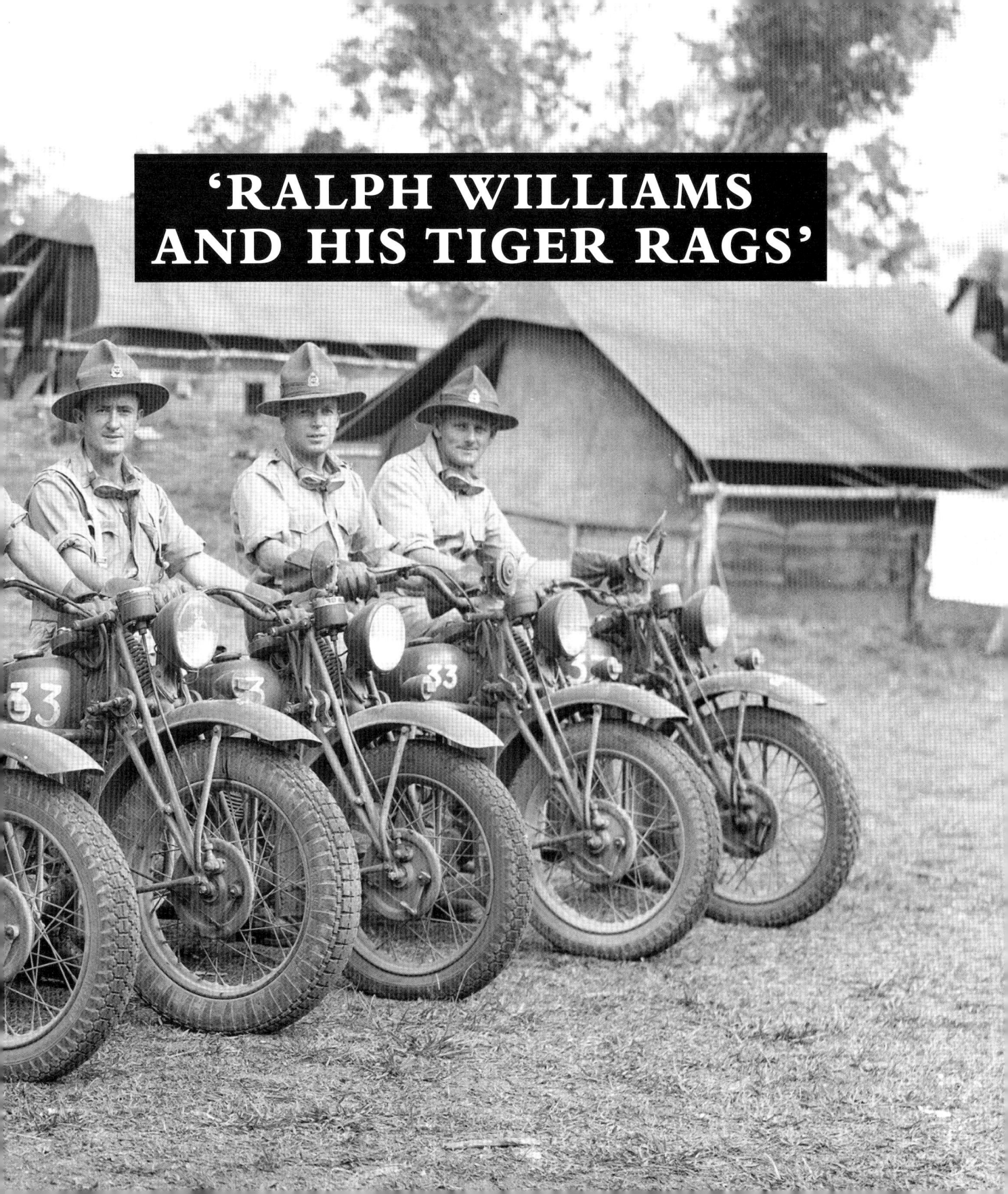

'RALPH WILLIAMS
AND HIS TIGER RAGS'

RALPH WILLIAMS, 409834,
SIGNALMAN, DIVISIONAL SIGNALS

Ralph Williams, the son of Claude and Eileen Williams, was born in Christchurch in 1920. Both his parents were music teachers, and Ralph briefly learnt the piano from his mother. After leaving Christchurch Technical College he was apprenticed as a tinsmith, the trade in which he was working when he was conscripted into the Territorials after his 21st birthday in 1941. He recalls being excited at the thought of going to war.

I WAS REALLY QUITE EXCITED and wondering what was going to eventuate. When the war broke out I wasn't very old and I wrote away to the Defence Department to see if I could get in the Parachute Corps. Anyway, my dear mother got to hear about it and that was the end of that, for which I'm so grateful. I probably wouldn't be here now. So she did me a great favour, actually. I had to wait until I was called up. My mother was against me going away, she put the kibosh on it, so I had to wait until I was 21 until I was finally called up to do my stuff. Lots of friends went away in the First Echelon. I was very keen to be with them.

Ralph was first posted to Riccarton racecourse near Christchurch, where he trained as a motorcycle despatch rider in Divisional Signals. In 1942 he was transferred to Blenheim, where he met his future wife, Phyllis Young.

Did you know when you met her that she was special?
Not really. I just got to know her, developed a friendship, and I used to walk her home. When I got

Previous page: *Despatch riders with their motorbikes, probably in New Caledonia.* ATL, War History Collection, WH-0151
Above: *Ralph Williams in Egypt in 1945.* Ralph Williams collection

En route to Vella Lavella from Guadalcanal. ATL, War History Collection, WH-0160

over to the islands in the Pacific I used to write to her every day. I've still got all the letters in an old suitcase. She wrote to me and sent me lovely biscuits regularly, home-made biscuits. They were called Sante biscuits, with bits of chocolate in them. I used to look forward to it.

Mail day was one of the most exciting events of all. We used to really look forward to it, and many a chap was disappointed because he didn't get any mail from home.

In early 1943 Ralph left New Zealand aboard USS West Point *with 3 Division bound for New Caledonia. In August that year he moved on to Guadalcanal in the Solomon Islands. He was not very taken with his camp there.*

The place had an atmosphere of death. When we established camp we were digging up skulls and things like that, which wasn't very good—rather bizarre. In the end people were hanging them in their tents. I don't know whether they were American skulls or Japanese. There'd been big battles going on there before we got there.

Was there one in your tent?

There was one in our tent. I didn't like it much. It hung right by the door where you went in. Above the door. I don't know what the idea of it was. I think I got rid of it in the end. It didn't appeal to me.

Troops packed onto the transport taking them to Vella Lavella.
Ralph Williams collection

I threw it down a hole somewhere. I thought they were barbaric.

But anyway, what fascinated me was the first night we had an air raid. All the searchlights were going up, big American 90-millimetre anti-aircraft guns firing. It was the first time I'd ever heard them. Most impressive. The searchlights picked up the silver plane, a Japanese bomber, away up. And then all of a sudden you heard this roar. Taking off from Henderson airfield were P-38s—Lightnings—American fighters. Up after the Japanese. And they finally got him.

Did you go outside and watch it or did you get into some kind of shelter?

We got out and watched every minute of it, intrigued with it all. It felt like we were getting a bit nearer, getting in the thick of it. We were highly excited about it.

As soon as we established camp, the first thing we'd do was dig a foxhole. We were issued with little wee shovels. It was a pretty hard job, hard ground. A lot of it was coral. The foxhole was just a shallow thing to lie in, a bit of protection.

The most frightening experience I had was an odd one, because we were out in the invasion barge off the coast of Vella Lavella. We were going to Munda with an American crew. We had a machine gun mounted in the stern. We were fully exposed out there. It was only a very small vessel. These Japanese Zeros flew over. They came over low. I thought, Hello, we're in for it. The old Yankee got up with the big machine gun, but he never fired a shot. I'm glad he didn't. The planes just flew right over. All

I could think was that they never had any ammunition. They'd been on a raid somewhere and they were flying home. That was a very uncanny experience. I thought we'd had it. There were about five of them in the flight. We wouldn't have had a dog's hope.

Did anyone say anything as they approached?

No. I think everyone was shaking. Nothing much was said. There was no shelter. We were in these open invasion barges. You sat there and shivered. I guess one or two prayed. It was quite a tense moment. I was glad when it was all over.

Ralph had some contact with Japanese prisoners of war while in the Solomon Islands.

I saw a Japanese with a great big gaping wound covered in blowflies. That was on Nissan Island. And what happened was the blowflies ate all the pus and kept the wound clean, and that probably saved his arm.

He was in a compound, and I saw another prisoner there. He was badly burnt. He was a pilot obviously and got shot down in flames, and he was very aggressive. I can still see him to this day. He was shouting and screaming, obviously in pain, very badly burnt. That stuck in my memory. He had some burns all over the body. A terrible mess. I did feel for him, because he must have been in terrible pain. The Japs were looked after by the Allies better than the Allies were looked after by the Japanese. We all know that.

How long would they be in those compounds for?

Oh, not very long. A couple of days, if that.

What was it like seeing Japanese behind netting like that?

It was better than seeing them lying on the ground bloated up after being killed. They used to get inflated like a football. The air seemed to blow their bodies up. The smell of decaying flesh—I can always remember that, which wasn't very nice. I'd far sooner see them alive and in a compound than shot on the ground.

They mainly had their pants and puttees and shirts, and they had a different sort of a helmet than we had. They had little caps, sort of jungle caps.

New Zealanders after landing on the beach at Vella Lavella. Ralph Williams collection

You form your own conclusions. I mean, they were just ordinary men. They had mothers and families back home. That's the sort of feeling you had towards them. You didn't feel bitter or anything like that. Well, I didn't.

How did you feel about the Japanese in general at that time?
I didn't feel hate towards them. Nothing like that. Never entered my head.

How do you think the other chaps felt?
Some were pretty horrible. I always remember, I think it was Vella Lavella and we were asked to go around where the Japanese had been and find out if any were left. A mopping-up exercise. We had to go through the jungle and we had stuff on us to make ourselves inconspicuous—burnt chalk to camouflage ourselves. A man felt a bit of a goat, in a way, but we went. We came through the jungle to a sort of bivouac where the Japanese had been, and it had one survivor. This poor emaciated little fellow, a Japanese soldier, the only one in the camp. And someone just shot him. I felt awful. To see a bloke shoot the Japanese. He had no weapon, nothing. And that really hit me hard. I said, 'Look, no need to do that. He was defenceless, he had nothing.'

Some were highly delighted that he'd knocked him off, but I felt it was awful because he was so pathetic, half-starved, and he had no weapon. I didn't like that one little bit. I wasn't the only one who felt that way.

Most of the time Ralph enjoyed being in the Pacific.

Those islands used to grow on you. Something about them was very appealing. Although you had a lot of time on your hands, you never got bored. There were such beautiful things there, and the lovely sea. It was so warm, lovely natives. They were lovely people, the Melanesians. Very down to earth and very useful. They knew all the movements of the Japanese.

In Vella Lavella, when we first landed we were establishing our camp and weren't far away from an Australian naval officer. He was based there on his own as a coastwatcher. They did a sterling job, because they were there on those islands well ahead of the Allied forces. Watching the Japanese movements and relaying the messages back by Morse code to base.

This particular naval officer was a nice guy, he had a great big beard, and had his naval ranking up on his shoulders. He had a thing like a bike and was pedalling away. There was a dynamo generating power so the coastwatcher could operate his Morse code key sending messages back. That really fascinated me. The native Solomon Islander was looking after the naval officer, like a batman I suppose you'd call him. Doing all his little chores for him. The islander was doing all his washing for him too. It was fantastic. He was attached to the Australian navy.

What was the attitude of the local Melanesian people towards the Japanese?
They hated them. They didn't want the Japanese at all, oh no. They hated the Japanese.

In September 1943 Ralph took part in the opposed landing at Joroveto Bay on Vella Lavella.

I remember riding the old Indian motorbike down the ramp of the LST onto the shore and into the jungle. The roads were absolute quagmires. There was a dogfight going on overhead by the RNZAF. They had Kittyhawks—we called them Warhawks in those days. They were engaging the Zeros attacking the landing. I was stuck in the damned road with this motorbike, but I found a beautiful American shovel and managed to dig myself out. Lucky I did. God must have put it there. I dug the thing out and got it going again and I roared off. I had the wind up with these things fighting over the top of me. It was really exciting.

I lost one of my best mates there. He was a Bofors anti-aircraft gunner and he got killed. That was a pretty tough landing.

Were you scared?

Yes. Oh yes. If you didn't feel scared you wouldn't be human, really.

Anyone smoke?

Smoking like chimneys. Actually they encouraged you to smoke in those days. We had an army issue of cigarettes, mainly Chelsea cigarettes. They were put in a peanut tin and sealed. About 100 cigarettes to a tin, and we were told we could smoke as many as we liked. We must have been going about 50 cigarettes a day, easy. When we landed at Vella Lavella, for the first two days we lived on cigarettes and coconut juice. The coconuts were beautiful, you knocked them off the palm tree and drank the milk. That's all we had the first two days. We had K rations, but we liked coconut juice and cigarettes.

> *While the landing was opposed, there were no troops on the ground. All the fire was coming from Japanese Zero fighters. Ralph felt the landing was chaotic.*

I had no idea what I was going to do. No idea whatsoever. It was every man for himself, more or less. I had no idea what was going to happen. It was a strange feeling, and as I say, I got bogged down. There wasn't much order. It was a bit worrying at the time, but actually it couldn't have lasted very long, though it seemed to while you were there experiencing it. I rode back to the beach to find out what was going on.

Could you see wounded lying around?

Yes, I could. Yes, I remember that quite vividly. That's when I found out that my friend had got it. I felt very upset about it. I really did; very upset. It hits you between the eyes, that happening to people you know. Your mates.

Immediately we had to dig a big hole in the ground for the radio, the cipher office. In the Signals they had the cipher office, coding and decoding messages. That was our first job: dig the big hole and put logs over the top in case of air raids. Dig ourselves foxholes and get ourselves established. I can remember putting a great big coconut palm log over the top for a roof, to give it stability and keep it protected. It was all hands on deck for doing that job. It was very important to get that established, to get proper communications. It was the main communications centre for the whole brigade. While they were doing all that I came into contact with the coastwatcher, because he wasn't very far away in his little camp. I must have gone for a bit of a look round, being a bit inquisitive, and in a new environment.

What else did you have to do when you were setting up camp?
We had to go and help form tracks through the jungle. The main thing was laying telephone cables. On Vella Lavella there wasn't much despatch-riding going on for a start and they got me in the cable gang. I remember they had great big drums of telephone cable which weighed about 100 pounds, and my job was to take my turn at putting it on my back and sort of trawl with the jolly thing. We had a sergeant in front of us leading the way, paying out the cable off our backs, so there would be communication with headquarters. We went right around the island. It took two or three days. It was a great experience. We cabled right around the island, to make contact with all the various camps.

It was pretty dense; real proper jungle, beautiful hardwood trees. We had machetes or jungle knives, and the sergeant was hacking his way through making a track. We used to follow him, playing out this cable. There was the odd clearing here and there. Sometimes they had Melanesian guides, because they knew every inch of the way. We'd call them black trackers. We weren't experienced. We weren't infantry, we were just signallers. It was scary, then again intriguing. An adventure. Everybody should have that. If they haven't, life's not worth much, is it?

Was there any expectation that there could be a Japanese ambush?
Yes, we had that in mind all the time. We were most apprehensive about that. There might be little pockets of Japanese on the island—which there were. We were vulnerable to them, although we were sort of guarded. We had soldiers with us ready for any sort of a contact, keeping an eye on things, which we were glad of.

> *After this period of cable-laying Ralph began despatch-riding in a jeep.*

Vella Lavellan guides and New Zealand troops, 1943.
ATL, War History Collection, WH-0248

In the islands it was mainly just daytime runs to the various camps. The roads were getting established by then. The roads used to deteriorate after a tropical downpour. They'd pack up straight away, but dry out quickly. The army engineers were always maintaining them. They were doing a great job looking after the roads there.

It rained. All of a sudden it would come out of the blue. It would pour. Come down in bucketsful. The next minute it would dry up and the sun would be shining and it would be a beautiful day.

Tell me about the band that you started.

In our tent, it started. There was a little fellow they called 'Pancho' for a nickname and he was quite good on the Hawaiian guitar, and another chap was interested in the old slap bass, and I was interested in the drums. Anyway, we decided to see if we could do something about it. So I made a bit of a drum, made a couple of drumsticks. This chap got an old tea chest and made a slap bass with a bit of cord, and we got a bit of a tune going. Chap had a mouth organ and we formed this little band, a quartet. They called it Ralph Williams and his Tiger Rags. We got so good that the CO said, 'We've got old Halsey coming.' [Admiral William] Halsey was the Allied commander for the Yanks, and we had a little bit of a do, a concert. That was good, went well. And a proper American dance drummer came, and he turned the drums inside out—couldn't he play! He made me feel rather inferior. He was an expert drummer, whereas I was only an amateur. Apparently Halsey enjoyed it.

Can you remember any of the numbers that you played?

'The Tiger Rag.' 'In the Mood.' All those sort of things. Nothing flash. Only what we could think of. We never had much of a repertoire. Our repertoire just came out of our head.

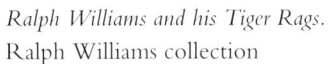

Ralph Williams and his Tiger Rags.
Ralph Williams collection

Signallers use climbing irons for their official purpose, as opposed to picking coconuts. ATL, War History Collection, WH-0354

How often did you play together?

As often as we could. We had plenty of time. It was all therapeutic. We enjoyed it.

Did you learn how to climb coconut trees?

I became quite an expert, but not as good as the Melanesians. They could shin up barefooted, but we used climbing irons strapped onto our legs. They had spikes and we could dig in. They belonged to the signallers for going up lamp posts. You had a safety belt to wrap around so you wouldn't fall. When you got to the top of some coconut palms you found white scorpions, which are rather frightening. Their tail used to come up ready to attack. They were about as big as your index finger.

We had a machete, or jungle knife, to knock the coconuts off the tree. When we got the juice out it was quite cold, being insulated by the shell of the coconut. It was just like drinking out of a fridge. I've never known anything to be so naturally sweet in all my life. It was a beautiful flavour. Inside the actual nut there's a wee white kernel, and that was lovely and tender to eat.

Another thing that used to fascinate me was the giant land crabs. Big, huge, as big as the size of the two palms of your hand, crawling towards the base of these coconut trees. They were terrific things. I suppose you could eat them if you wanted to. We never thought of eating them, but you could, I suppose, if you were starving. They never bothered us, but they used to fascinate us.

The ants were bad news. Bull ants. They used to bite and sting, sort of nip you. They'd be about the size of a little fingernail. They were long in the body, a bulbous shape, and they were red. Peculiar things. This is fascinating. You'd see a great big leaf and you'd wonder why the leaf was moving, and you'd have a look closer and you'd see scores of ants under this leaf propelling it along on the ground. There must have been marvellous intelligence there.

At the end of 1943, Ralph and his unit moved to Nissan Island, north of Bougainville.

What were you doing as signalmen on Nissan?
Mainly driving jeeps and taking despatches. We did patrols now and again, but that was mostly done by the infantry battalion. They were going through the jungle, seeing off any remnants of Japanese, things like that.

One of my highlights was a flight on a Liberator bomber. The Americans were very generous. You had to sign a form to take all responsibility off the flyers in case anything happened. You had to sit in an air gunner's position, a waist gunner, on a Liberator bomber. They're a big four-engine aircraft. That happened on Vella Lavella. I was determined to get a flight so I drove along to the American flight headquarters, being a cheeky scrounging Kiwi, and asked the Americans, 'Any chance of getting a flight?' He said, in his American accent, 'Yeah, OK. You sign this paper.' So I did. In a Liberator bomber, B-24.

The two American pilots were half-naked, only had shorts on. They were both smoking cigars flying the goddam thing. It went over Truk Island in the Pacific and it was loaded with bombs. I had a wonderful experience. Came back safely. I hoped and prayed no blimmin' Zeros poked their noses in.

Would you have known what to do?
I'd pull the trigger, don't know what I'd be firing at. Anyway, we got back safely.

A 'puddle jumper' quad bogged in the lagoon on Nissan Island. Ralph Williams collection

The Americans tended to just abandon equipment, didn't they?

Oh yes. Most wasteful, but the American industrial might was terrific. Once they got going in the war, nothing would stop them. They kept building all these things.

How did the New Zealanders compare in terms of equipment?

We were very conservative. Everything had high value, it didn't matter what it was. Any kind of ordnance, anything at all, anything that moved—or anything that didn't move—was highly valued and looked after, well maintained.

I never really got bored, time went along quite well, but I was always wanting to get home. I was always homesick. The time came when they came around and asked if anyone wanted to go home. I said, 'Yes. My mother has infantile paralysis and she's not very well and I would like to go home and see her.' They said, 'Right, you can get away a bit earlier than the others.' So I got away about a month or two ahead. I went to New Caledonia base camp and got home from there.

I was very glad to land at the wharf in Auckland. There were girls there waiting, and as soon as they knew that we belonged to 3 Div they weren't interested. That's the comparison between the two divisions, you see. In 2 Div they get all the glory—the desert and Italy and all that. But 3 Div, we weren't

New Zealanders peel potatoes in New Caledonia. ATL, War History Collection, WH-0782

quite so active. They didn't want to be bothered with us. It didn't worry us. We went straight to the Papakura Camp, and opened a bottle of DB beer.

> *During this time Ralph got engaged to Phyllis. He was then posted to the Middle East for nine months, but did not take part in any fighting. He returned to New Zealand and married in 1946. The couple have three children. Ralph finished his tinsmith apprenticeship and worked in the trade after the war.*

What are your feelings now about the service that you gave in the Pacific?
I'm so glad that I didn't miss it. I'm glad of the experience and the wonderful confidence that I gained.

Ralph Williams is welcomed home after his return from the Middle East. Ralph Williams collection

Before I went to the war, I was a bad stutterer. I never had much confidence. I don't know why I stuttered, whether it was a nervous complaint. But I got over that. After the war it was a whole new ball game. Ralph Williams was the boss. I was a changed man. No more stuttering, more confidence, and ready to carry on with life and do my best. The war never did me any harm. I was so grateful, and lucky, to come out unscathed.

'WE STRAFED DOWN THE JUNGLE'

RICHARD MAPP, NZ4311331,
FLIGHT SERGEANT,
ROYAL NEW ZEALAND AIR FORCE

Dick Mapp was born in Morrinsville in the Waikato in 1923 and grew up on the family farm. He was called up at the age of 18 and posted to 9 Field Ambulance, which was based near Kaikohe in Northland. After around 15 months Dick enlisted in the air force, because he felt he would not get overseas otherwise. He recalls the send-offs for men going overseas from the Morrinsville area.

I N THE DISTRICT OF WALTON we had a public hall, and there was always a dance-type send-off, with those who were going being the guests of honour. There was always a band, usually a three- or four-piece. There was a piano in the hall, always a violin, and there'd be drums and usually something else. But there were several bands around who used to come on request.

The servicemen were in civvies normally, unless they happened to be on their final leave. Then, of course, they would be in uniform. It was very much a case of the men standing on one side of the hall and the women sitting down on the other. People really enjoyed themselves once they got into the dancing, and then there would be supper. There would be speeches after supper. I can't really remember them. I can only say that the person was held up for being brave and doing the right thing.

Was there any sense that these men were going away possibly to be killed?
The possibility was in everybody's mind, but they were expected to go and do a job. That was the way we thought of it at the time.

Previous page: *RNZAF Corsairs off Guadalcanal, 1944.* ATL, Evatt Collection, F-106417-1/2
Above: *Dick Mapp, 1942.* Richard Mapp collection

Dick recalls being called up and sent to the field ambulance in January 1942.

I had to catch a train to Whangarei, and I was posted to 9 Field Ambulance. I had no option, and I was horrified because field ambulance people were conchies and I wasn't. I applied to get out of it, but I wasn't allowed to.

Why do you think they put you in there?

They were setting up teams to cover the North Auckland area in case of invasion, and they had to have the field ambulances. They took the whole of one draft and put them into it.

There was only a basic core of 9 Field Ambulance at that time. They had been drafted from another field ambulance. There were about 20 of them who were NCOs and officers, and they brought us in and trained us. But all the ones that came in on our draft were not conscientious objectors.

All our officers were doctors, and they were not conscientious objectors. But of our NCOs quite a number were, and also later on when we required additional numbers, they came in as conscientious objectors. One of our members was a young man, one of the largest young men I've ever seen, and he went out of camp one night and got horribly drunk, so drunk that he couldn't really stand up or do anything. He came back to camp and was going to 'kill him a conchie'. We almost had to tie him down to stop him. There were about 10 of us holding him down to prevent him getting into trouble with the CO.

Dick did not particularly enjoy his time in the field ambulance.

I really wanted to get more into the war. This war was going on and I wasn't doing anything. That was how I felt.

Why the air force?

Dare I say it? Glamour, I suppose. There was a lot of news about the air war at that time, and I think that must have persuaded me to join up then.

What sort of process did you have to go through to get out of the army and into the air force?

You simply sent away a form, I don't even remember now how I got it, and they shortly afterwards sent back to say yes, you've been accepted, you'll be advised of a posting date later. It happened quite quickly.

They gave me a written test to see what my education was, but I hadn't had any senior high school at all. I only had one year at high school, but they did accept me on that basis, because they were really looking for pilots at that time.

Dick left the army in August 1943 and began air force training. In April 1944 he began flying training on Tiger Moths at Ashburton. He continued training on Harvard, Kittyhawk (P-40) and Corsair aircraft at Woodbourne airbase. He was posted to Ohakea in January 1945 and joined 20 Squadron at Whenuapai in May. 20 Squadron was a fighter-bomber squadron flying Corsairs.

The squadron did about a fortnight's practice training from Ardmore, and we used to do a lot of low flying over the Hauraki Gulf. That was quite good fun. The lower you could get down at times the better, and I've seen planes leaving a wake on the water without actually touching it. The blast from the propeller was creating the wake. We must have only been two or three feet above the water. We used to do quite a lot of formation flying across the water. You could see the other person leaving the wake when you were side by side. You knew you must have been doing the same.

We left from Whenuapai in a Douglas Dakota. The whole squadron.

What was the flight like?

Long, boring. They were very uncomfortable planes because they were not set up as passenger planes. They were just an empty cargo hold, really. We knew we were going into the Pacific right from at least Ohakea days when we started on the P–40s. We flew from Whenuapai on May 21, from Espiritu Santo on the 22nd and we arrived in Green [Nissan] Island the same day.

It was just simply an airstrip carved out of the coral. Green Island is just a coral ring, quite a large ring, about 12 miles across apparently. There's the lagoon in the middle and just an opening at the far end. We got off the plane and stepped out onto the strip, and the whole thing was only about 500 yards wide including the strip. Other parts were much narrower than that. It was an American base. Their ships used to come into the lagoon, run right up to the coral reef, throw down a gangplank, and unload direct onto the coral from the ship.

On 27 May the squadron left Green Island for Jacquinot Bay on New Britain.

What was it like?

There was a harbour with a coral ring around it and an opening to allow ships and so forth to come in. There were wharves and stores and so forth built there. Everything that was coming in to New Britain came in through this port. There was a road up to our airstrip, which was just carved with a bulldozer out of the coral. In the jungle we had tents all scattered through.

Our job was to support the Australians whenever they had any problem and keep Rabaul, which was

These pilots are probably from 20 Squadron, Guadalcanal. RNZAF Official PR3405, via Air Force Museum, Christchurch

A Chance Vought Corsair lands at Jacquinot Bay, May 1945. RNZAF Official PR6754, via Air Force Museum, Christchurch

the major town of New Britain—occupied by the Japanese—keep it under control so that they couldn't do any major attacks from there against the Australian army. Harass the Japanese around the Rabaul area. There was a front line roughly halfway between Rabaul and Jacquinot Bay, and the Australians were facing up to the Japanese soldiers there.

The camp at Jacquinot Bay was a large rest camp for the Australian forces.

They had a lot of stores, a sawmill, and camps spread all through the area, and hospitals. It was a full set-up. I don't know how many soldiers were there. They used to come back and rest for a time, and somebody else would then go up into the front line.

It crossed your mind two or three times while there that, particularly in the early days, there could be a breakthrough, but nothing ever happened like that. They were just too closely guarded really. The Australians seemed to be doing a good job, and occasionally we would get called in to do a bombing strike along the front line.

We were given a tent for every six pilots. We very quickly found some more. They came from different places, mostly from the Australian army. I was once with a couple of other chaps sent out to get timber. We went down to the sawmill, took down three or four cartons of cigarettes and got a truckload of timber. This was used to build floors in our huts and build a framework for them. We turned our tents into huts. We built decking outside, a timber stand for our water drum. We set ourselves up quite well.

What was the temperature like?

It was winter but we never had anything below about 20 degrees, and up to round about 30. It was fairly even in temperature, but you'd be standing out in the sun and the sweat would just be pouring out of you, so we had our little shower rigged up. You'd change your clothes, and then if you went out in the sun again in another 10 minutes or quarter of an hour you'd be sweating again. Your clothes would be wringing wet.

It rained a lot. There were water pipes through the camps, and for our shower we tapped onto that so that we could have showers when we wanted, but we also put guttering along our tent and caught the rainwater as it came off. It ran into our little water tank which we used for washing clothes, because you were washing your clothes all the time. We also had what we called a cactus stove. We used to boil the billy and have our coffee and that sort of thing any time we wanted.

One of our pilots had a bright idea and brought a kerosene lantern, which we put into the bottom of a little cabinet, and this was our drying cabinet to keep our clothes so they didn't go mouldy. Three people had quite a bit of clothing and you needed to keep it all in there to keep it from going mouldy. Boots went mouldy overnight, grew white stuff. If you didn't put them on for two or three days then it got quite bad.

We used to have Atebrin for malaria. Daily.

Did you go yellow?

Yes. Quite yellow. We used to take salt tablets, too. They were quite large and you took two each morning at breakfast. They'd be roughly about as big as a peppermint. You swallowed them with water.

It was the rainy season for that area and we had huge rainfall. We had 17 inches in 24 hours once. We couldn't do any flying at all. Nobody took off in that whole time. Muddy. Muddy, muddy, muddy. It was a surface of mud on top of the coral.

We used to maintain a patrol over Rabaul as long as it was possible to fly in the weather, from daylight till dark. We had two pilots up there all the time, and it was their job to search out any activity that was going on, and if anything was found you would send up bombing strikes to pound it. That's what we did.

When you went on a Rabaul patrol, you had two hours on once a day when you were doing that. It took you about 40 minutes to get up there and 40 minutes to come home, so that took about three and a half hours. Then by the time you did your report back at base afterwards, it took about four hours in total. So you had to get up about an hour before daylight if you were on the first patrol, to get ready and be up there by daylight.

Muddy, muddy, muddy. This is on Mono Island in 1943. ATL, War History Collection, F–44803-1/2

I wasn't scared of being captured because I didn't feel I would be.

Were you given any training about what to do if you were captured?

Not a lot. You were advised of the rights you had and what you must say and must not say. And that's about it. All you could do was give your name, rank, and number. And you must not volunteer or give any other information at all. Not your squadron, not any of the people you worked with, or anything like that.

Could you communicate with the other plane you were flying with?

Yes, you could. You had a microphone which was sitting by your mouth on a little frame from the back of the helmet. You had goggles. You had hot and cold air blowers, which could help, and you could open your canopy a little bit to get yourself a bit of air, to cool down. The rush of air going past you was a bit of a problem, it was pretty noisy.

Were you ever shot at?

Yes. It must have been a fairly heavy machine gun, because right in front of me was a burst of little things. They were bullets. You could see them coming. They went right up in front of me. I could hear the gun discharging down below. Fortunately, it shot in front of me.

We were bombing a dump. The Japanese had cut a tunnel through a hill, open both ends, and we were given the job of trying to get bombs to go down the tunnel and blow the whole thing up. It was surrounded by ack–ack machine-gun fire, fairly heavy machine-gun fire. We each had two delayed-fuse bombs so that they would go off inside the tunnel, if you were so good that you actually hit the tunnel. Several of them did, and the others were plastered around it as well. We cleaned up the tunnel. It was smashed up.

I'd just dropped my bomb and fortunately for me I was just going to pull away, so it probably put me out of the range of that particular shooter. You could hear the guns going off above the sound of your engine, but you never knew whether they were shooting at you or not, so after that run you came around and did another run. I don't think that was being brave, it was just you had this to do and you did it. You had your instructions and everybody else did the same. I mean, you wouldn't have dreamt of not going in.

Did you ever think that the bombs were likely to kill people?

That's why you were doing it. I didn't hear anybody say that they had a problem with doing that.

What was the feeling about the Japanese at that time among the men that you were flying with?

We thought they were horrible little men. They were nasties and you had to do what you could to stop them because of the way they had treated the prisoners they had taken and the way they had fought in the jungle.

The very first day that I did a flight on duty, two of us were sent up to bomb and strafe an area along a river. The Australians were on one side of it and the Japs were on the other side. They had some barges, and the Australians asked for them to be knocked out. We went up there and couldn't find the barges at all, so then we just dropped our bombs on the Japanese side of the river and strafed down the jungle. All you could see was jungle. I mean, you didn't know what you were doing really, but we had the ammunition and we were there, so why not do something, make a show?

A bomb-laden Corsair taxis away from the line at Piva airstrip, Bougainville, 1945. RNZAF Official PR5752, via Air Force Museum, Christchurch

Dick explains when the machine guns on the plane were used.

They were used for air-to-ground shooting at Japanese. This was part of Rabaul patrol. You'd see one of their trucks and you'd tear down and try and shoot it up. They had canoes which they used to carry stuff up and down the coast. We used to shoot them up. Anything. If we saw tents or a camp we'd shoot into that. You could tell that they were being hit. Also trucks—they usually went on fire.

Usually you'd start off about 1500 feet, that was the standard bombing run, and then you'd come down if we were doing daisycutters, which were the ones that had a tube out the front and had instant detonation, so that the thing actually burst above ground level. You would see it clear the jungle, see

Rabaul, showing the township and Simpson harbour. Australian War Memorial, Neg. 096796

the blast run through the jungle as it went off. You couldn't come down below about 800 or 900 feet, otherwise you'd get shrapnel from your own bomb. When we were ground strafing we'd be down to 50 feet quite commonly. You couldn't see a great deal; you couldn't see anything really, you're simply going too fast over the ground, but you can see stuff that's 400 or 500 yards in front. You line up on that and then when you get within range you can start shooting.

In your windscreen in front of you, you had your gunsight. It was actually a red light which was set onto the windscreen and calibrated. If you were sitting in the right place in your plane and you put that dot on your target, that's where your bullets would hit.

On the Rabaul patrol you'd go up with your partner as a pair; one straight behind the other, not too far away. Twenty or 30 yards away at most. When you got there, you would each go your own way but you would keep a close eye on your friend so that you always knew what he was doing. The lead man would perhaps say, 'We'll go down and have a look at so and so now', and you would go off with him. When we went up as a bombing strike we would fly as a whole group together. The lead man would have one plane on his left and there would be two on his right. If an attack came they would break up, and the two pairs would then operate together as cover for each other.

Dick recalls bombing Japanese camps around Rabaul.

We would drop daisycutter bombs which would blow the camp and the jungle about quite badly. You could see a ripple go right out through the jungle for quite a long way, a compression ripple from the blast. That blast would eventually catch up with you, you'd feel it on your plane even if you were quite high.

You had to fly the best you could. You had to use skill that you had attained and from the things that we were doing, we seemed to be doing satisfactorily without it being risky. We had a scoresheet which was done up at the end of the tour. Canoes and barges, small craft, trucks, Japs, huts, cars, tunnels, gun positions damaged or destroyed.

How did you know that you'd killed Japanese?
Sometimes if you turned around and came back again you would see them lying, and other times it would have to be an estimate. If it was a troop-carrying truck it would just have to be an estimate. If it

was a supply truck you would normally consider two people in that.

We were going up the east coast of New Britain and a lot of ships were calling into there. There was nothing much except barges and canoes around Rabaul itself, because that was all Japanese-held.

What could you see on the ground in Rabaul?

Mainly jungle, and here and there there were airstrips, and some buildings. As far as possible they put service buildings under the trees so that they were less visible. In an area where the Americans had come over with a big bombing strike, as they did from time to time, there would be huge bomb holes in the ground. Gradually they would seem to get filled up again. I suppose the Japanese would do it.

Very seldom did you go in the same plane twice running. It would depend what planes were available, we didn't each have our own particular plane. We had about 20 planes for the squadron and there were usually two or three being serviced, so the most we could get out at one time would probably be about 16, from 26 people in the squadron. There were two squadrons of us, only one lot of groundcrew. There were about 250 of them, and 50 pilots altogether.

What did you do in the evenings?

We played a lot of cards, a tremendous amount of cards. A lot of poker, threepenny bets. You could get books from the YMCA library—general books, novels, but not a lot of them.

Did you ever get movies?

I think we only had two in the time that I was there. We had a gully in a coconut plantation, and they'd cut all the coconut trees down and made the seats in an amphitheatre, an open-air one. It was a mobile screen, and we sat on the stumps watching it across the gully.

There were local people in the area of the camp at Jacquinot Bay.

Some of them couldn't speak any English at all, others could. There were a few that used to hang around the camp. One of them told me they had some huts down past the sawmill. They used to come through the camp and scrounge what they could. They had very lightly built bodies. I didn't see any fat ones. There would be some women and even a few children, but the women and children

Airmen with Jacquinot Bay locals, 1945. RNZAF Official PR6758, via Air Force Museum, Christchurch

wouldn't come into the camp. They would try and slip by, past the camp. The men were quite happy
to come through the camp.

How much news did you get about the rest of the war?

A little bit, major things. Not a lot. The end of the war, when it came, seemed to be very quick from our point of view, because we hadn't heard much and then all of a sudden we got the very sharp command, Get packed up now, from the Squadron Leader. He got a plane, a Dakota, to take us back home again. We knew we were due to go out in about a week's time because our three months would have been up then, but he was very much afraid that the war would end and instead of being taken back in the normal course of events we would be kept there, so he shot us home as fast as he could. We flew back again to Espiritu Santo. There was a sadness about it, certainly. You did seem to be leaving your own little nest. I enjoyed the flying, the control of the plane and seeing things from the air. It was something I liked doing.

We didn't go back to Green Island, just flew directly to Espiritu Santo and then next day back to New Zealand.

What was the homecoming like for you?

I was looking forward to getting home and seeing the people at home. Once we left Santo on the last leg, I couldn't get there quick enough. We got there about seven o'clock at night as I remember, it was dark. We had a quick medical and were put into barracks for the night, and then we had a full medical the next day. Then we were allowed to go on leave, so I could slip home to Mum, who was just out of Auckland.

> *In 1946 Dick married his first wife, Fay, whom he had met while doing air training in Ashburton. The couple farmed near Matamata before moving to Christchurch, where Dick still lives with his second wife, Betty.*

'JAPANESE
IN LARGE NUMBERS'

ALAN ROBERTS, 90636, LIEUTENANT, LONG-RANGE AIR WARNING RADAR

Alan Roberts was born in Timaru in 1921. He attended Timaru Boys' High School and then Canterbury University College, where he studied radiophysics for a BSc. In 1941, still a student at Canterbury, he volunteered to join the army special artillery unit. Because of his radiophysics studies, however, he was transferred to a radar unit and posted to Godley Head, near Christchurch.

Did you have any particular interest in radiophysics?

No, not particularly, but it was explained to us that we could be useful for gunnery, for communications. The radar is a radio wave of a certain frequency which they beam out, it hits a solid object and comes back, and by knowing the speed of the wave and by measuring the time before it came back onto the screen you could figure out how many miles out the object was. The government decided to cover all the coastal batteries.

I think there were only perhaps half a dozen of us at that stage. Then they set up this special laboratory in Wellington, which was originally Post & Telegraph communication and then became a radar lab. It was protected by the army. You had to have passes to get into it. All the departments were separate, to the extent that it depended on what wavelength of radar you were working on. There was a 10-centimetre and there was something more like a metre wavelength. These rays had different penetrating ability, but so that no one scientist knew too much they all worked in separate departments and you never really knew what was going on. It was all top secret at that stage.

We were suddenly tossed into servicing radar plants and radar equipment, keeping it working after Japan entered the war. It was breaking down an awful lot and they were refining it as they went along.

Previous page: *Loading the radar trucks for Guadalcanal.* Alan Roberts collection
Above: *Alan Roberts.* Alan Roberts collection

Alan Roberts is third from right, second row from back, 1941. Alan Roberts collection

I was living in Wellington and hating every minute, because of being a civilian and everybody eyeing you up and down. When you went out onto a station, be it army or air force, there was a fair degree of suspicion: he looks fit and well. How the hell's he managing to escape army duty? You got to know the people you were working with, and got along reasonably well, but it meant that when everybody else was going to the canteen at night you tended to stick in your room and read. You couldn't attend the various things, simply because you'd cause too much of a problem as a civilian.

Alan remembers the development of the mobile long-range air warning radar units in Wellington.
After capturing Guadalcanal, the commander of the South Pacific Area, US Vice-Admiral William

Halsey, planned the next move—the invasion of New Georgia—in his drive north through the Solomon Islands towards the Japanese base at Rabaul.

He needed equipment which could go on with his assault-wave troops. They were quite happy to have some sort of radar that would perch somewhere and give a red alert saying Japanese planes there, 26 miles off, which would just give them enough time to get into their foxholes. Consequently their casualty list was a hang of a lot less, because they weren't caught above ground by aeroplanes coming over the horizon low down. Some of the radar wouldn't pick them low down, but they couldn't travel the whole time low down so we'd pick them up 25 miles out and give the warning. So 1 Marine Division were very happy to have this with them, and that's how two of us ended up on Nissan.

So long as you could get it ashore and start your generator, put up an aerial, if you got a reasonable site you could be working in an hour instead of a day and a half to three days. The radar was on one truck, two generators in another truck.

Alan left New Zealand in December 1943 and spent a month at New Caledonia.

Staging, it's called. In other words, trying the machinery, making sure it was working, trying to find out what its range was, how high you could get to get a longer range. Collecting stores. Then it was off to Guadalcanal.

The unit trained with United States Navy Argus units, which were also radar units.

They were a bit ill at ease. They felt we were poaching their territory, but they had to do as they were told. If there was radar which could become more rapidly operative in the assault phase of the war, then they would do so. They were mainly about my age, mainly students, and therefore we could react on the same level, whereas the American Marines were professional soldiers and were a different breed altogether.

Once they found a ship we moved off to Guadalcanal.

Alan did not enjoy his time on Guadalcanal.

I think it was just living with fear. You never quite got used to it. It was as simple as that. Some places were lucky. Once they were cleared they could run movie shows at night quite happily with no problems. But wherever we were, there were still Japanese in large numbers. Peleliu in the Palau group, where I was later, had 11,000 or 12,000 Japs on it and it was only six miles by one mile, so it was a bit crowded by the time you put in another 20,000 American Marines. In Guadalcanal, it was the fear of the jungle at night.

You never know how you'll face up to something rough until it actually happens. My main fear was jungle warfare. Not of dying. It was fear of capture with a bounty on my head, because I'm sure I'd have been whimpering the moment they looked at me and giving all that I knew about. I felt I wouldn't have had the courage to stand it. And by that time, of course, we knew about what had happened to the Post & Telegraph people. They could have been brought back to New Zealand. I'm sure they could have done the same work using aircraft to do the surveillance for them instead of leaving these poor bastards in the middle of Japanese-held territory, knowing that they were going to be caught sooner or later.

Alan Roberts (right) with two Americans from the Argus unit. Alan Roberts collection

Alan is referring to the New Zealand coastwatchers who were captured by the Japanese in the Gilbert Islands, 17 of whom were subsequently beheaded on Tarawa.

How effective was the radar that you were running from these trucks?
It was very effective when we needed it. We were officially only there at night. The fleet was supposed to do it in the daytime, but there were so many of them around that there were many false blips—little

strokes that came on the radar that were friendly. The aircraft had IFF, which is 'Identification, Friend or Foe', another piece of radio equipment. Once our radar hit this thing it beamed back a signal which said it would only be a friendly aircraft. The Japs didn't have the equivalent at the time.

The men worked in shifts of four in the radar trucks.

They'd run for six hours. Some were a lot better than the others, so you'd leave them for the night. They would grizzle with a smile on their face. They were dedicated guys. I would tend to spend the nights with them. You learned to sleep sitting in a chair. Normally you fed the information through, if you had a landline, to a command centre, which sometimes they could set up on land; otherwise it would be to a ship standing off, by radio.

We could notify them of the distance and then you'd hear the siren going for a red alert which, on memory, gave you seven minutes to get yourself below ground level. We couldn't operate from below ground level. You could dig in a wee bit if you were right on the top of a hill, but if it was low down you had to have your trucks above it, otherwise you'd get no distance at all. We went searching for any bit of a mound. A few feet would give us a few miles; your horizon is that much further on.

How effective was the camouflage?
Seemingly not bad, because we never suffered any direct hits.

During a raid, what would you do?

Get in there and keep talking. If the landline went out we would try contacting the pilots directly and they would come in. We knew what the flight code names were. You could break silence if the plane was close enough. You maintained silence from a distance in case some of the other flights could get them, but once they got close enough you could break silence and talk.

You've got to operate in the dark with your screens. It was a bit claustrophobic. I don't remember any particular soundproofing. There was so much racket, it was always noisy and you'd feel the whole truck shake. Howitzers and mortars dropped close enough to shake you. The boys would have a look around when daylight came, and I think 10 yards was the closest to one hitting us. I don't know why they didn't do better on Nissan, except they hurriedly got out. They pushed these things through the hole in the mountain, fired them and then pulled them back again. Nissan was fairly straightforward. That was my first opposed landing.

What do you remember of the preparation for that?

That was fairly low key. It was not heavily opposed, so it was no particular problem. The worry of our lives was the diesel engines. The gear wasn't too bad at all and behaved very well. All electronic gear has faults and, until I got adequate ventilation, things packed up with heat. The highly secret parts were the big valves which developed the rays. They came from Britain and America, I think.

Did you have to do the repairs yourself?

Yes. We had some very good technicians there who had been in radio all their lives. When it came to putting them back together again those boys were far better. They'd been doing it all their lives, making small soldering joints and all sorts of things.

> *After time on Nissan Island, Alan returned to New Zealand for a fortnight's leave. In September 1944 he joined a United States Argus unit in the Palau group of islands, where he took part in the landing at Peleliu.*

Left: *Camouflaged radar trucks, Guadalcanal.* Alan Roberts collection

We were not troubled by aeroplanes. We'd had the kamikazes when we were getting close. Officially, you weren't allowed on deck. It was only because I knew the deck officers. They were busy, but they would let you up there provided you weren't a nuisance. I didn't feel so shut in. At one stage a guy called Martin asked me if I would navigate the ship. He had things to do. I said, 'God, you've got to be joking.' He said, 'Try and hold it on this bearing, and if you make a mistake I told the helmsman to bail you out.' It was only for about half or three-quarters of an hour, I suppose.

There were dozens of ships. Then they slowed down for a day because the navy had decided that they hadn't reduced the place to submission enough. We waited. I've never seen so much firepower in all my life. From the American navy. I think the initial waves would go in not long after daybreak. I think we all stood to at about five o'clock in the morning. They would have to get the first barge-loads off the beach to make room for the next. I think the first ones got off very rapidly because there wasn't a Jap in sight, but once they got inside the beach the Japanese just rained mortars and howitzers down on them.

We were standing off in the lagoon, could see through. If it was too bad they'd mobilise the rocket ships again. They had enormous anti-personnel power and they would put these salvos of rockets in quite accurately, perhaps 15 metres from the actual beach. That would enable the troops to move in a bit more and let the next ones in. We thought we were going in, and then some guy in a wee high-speed boat which was going back and forth in front of the various lines of troop carriers signalled not to move because he wanted to get everything ashore safely. I think it was three or four o'clock in the afternoon before we got in.

They had a great big ramp which dropped down. They'd just nudge in by beaching a boat, put the ramp down, and if it was very soft the CBs would put down some form of metal track. That's an LST. We were always told that once they cut the engines you went overboard into the water because you had the protection from at least one side of the vessel, which was quite thick armour, against rifle fire. The driver didn't. The driver had to drive on up, and then we had to join him and find the beach master, who would tell us where to go. He had a big red flag. If there'd been Japs up and about he would have been a sitting duck. He had a most unenviable job. The rest of them could at least hurry up and get themselves flat, or get themselves into some form of cover, or dig a foxhole, but he just had to stand, directing everybody. I've never admired anybody so much as that guy. He was a Marine major. It was actually very well organised. I was surprised at how well the logistics had been worked out.

An LST. This one is arriving at Vella Lavella. Ralph Williams collection

You waded in and joined your trucks and headed inland. We could put our gear in the trucks. We were told to mind our own business and leave the fighting to the Marines. Everything was happening and you really didn't have too much time to think about anything. I just hurried to where the red flag was. I wouldn't think it was more than perhaps 150 metres from the seashore to the jungle. I ran to the red flag, to this guy, and he pointed where to go. Then we scrambled up and stood on the side of the truck, as I remember, and the drivers gunned them. Once the truck was out of sight you could take a deep breath because you were off the beach. They'd had to send people in to blast all the booby-trapping. They had these great stakes pointing out to stop the landing vehicles getting through, and the navy diving teams, I presume, went in. Maybe much of it was exploded by the destroyers' firepower. They certainly made quite reasonable gaps where the boats could get through.

Were you aware of people being shot down around you?
Yes. But not shot down, downed by howitzers and mortars. Eight-inch howitzers would blow people up. They would flatten everybody within a 20- or 30-metre radius. They were brutes of things, they had enormous power. I don't know what they were loaded with, anti-personnel shells of some sort.

They were the real difficulty. They caused very severe woundings, and at that stage the medic teams were pretty much bound down as well.

How did they get the wounded off the beach?

Good question. I've no idea. I'm afraid you didn't turn round to look back, you just kept on going. The impression I have is that you were expendable at that stage. Later on they became more organised with getting their wounded back in, but not in the initial assault wave. You were expendable, and you just kept your fingers crossed.

I don't know whether there was a sense of relief. Initially, briefly, you were happy that you got there in one piece. Then the relief was when the trucks were working. You could take a deep breath and start making contact with the command centres.

Laying the lines to the command centres was difficult. Some poor signals wallahs had to go and do it. Somebody would bring in the line and say, 'Here it is.' The lines went out frequently. I think that was probably the shells.

The first thing was to camouflage the truck. You threw that over, and then you'd put your aerial up and put some more camouflage around it so it wasn't tangling, and there it was.

US sailors inside the mobile radar trailer, Peleliu. Alan Roberts collection

There were many Japanese on the island, and Alan often heard them at night.

They had raiding parties. You could hear them banzai-ing at night. They were stupid enough to shout, and consequently the boys would put a hail of bullets into the area where the noise was coming from. They declared themselves instead of creeping around in deadly silence. You could hear them, and you hoped that there were enough Marines out there to mow them down before they got close. We had no way of knowing how far away they were. You had to put your faith in someone, and I was just grateful that it was 1 Marine Division. I was quite pro-American, simply because I owe the Americans my life.

Who was bringing you the food?
I've got an idea that it was all K rations, but one of the boys would go and prepare it. You carried your own and used a pocket knife to open up the tins, and he would produce the hot drink for you.

Alan was wounded by a Japanese sniper while trying to rescue one of the men from the Argus team who had been shot.

My only memory is I could see him lying there with huge gunshot wounds, outside the truck. We were setting off to try and find a different place. I saw him go down and I vaguely remember seeing where it was coming from, but my last thoughts were, That's Cruz, I'm not going to leave him. That's really the last thing I remember particularly well. One of the Marines had

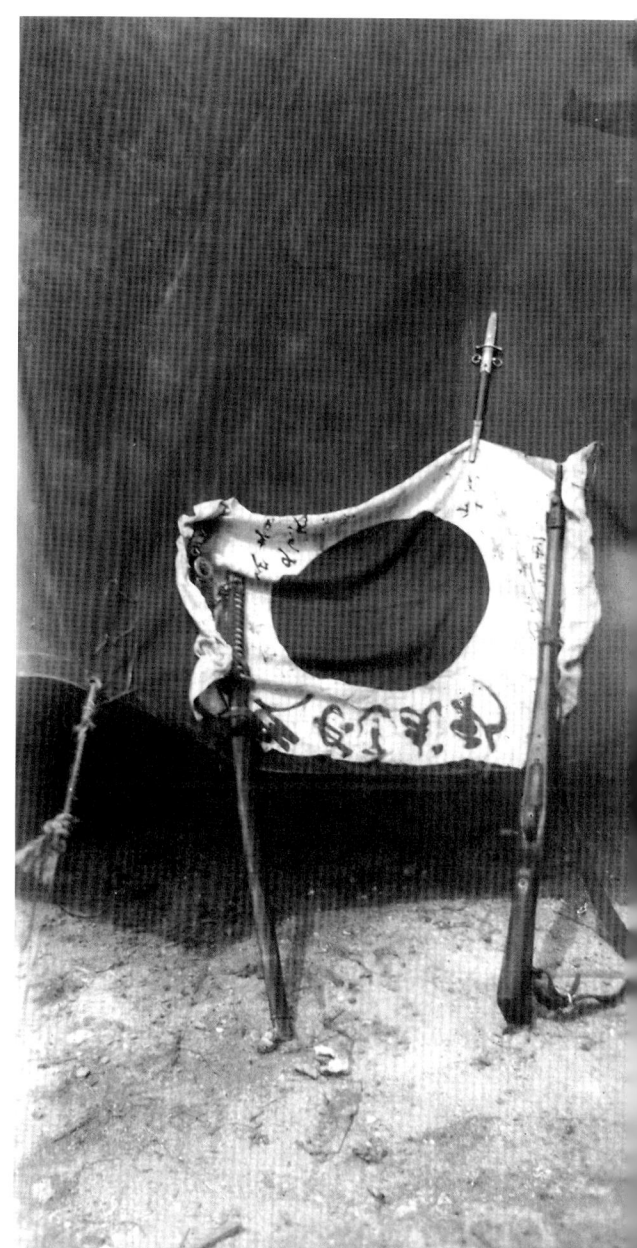

Japanese souvenirs from Peleliu. Alan Roberts collection

covered for me and he'd caught it in the hand, his hand was just about blown off. I remember being able to walk back as far as one of the aid posts. I must have been directed there. I realised I'd been hit in the chest and I felt OK. There was a lot of blood around. Then I heard an American voice saying, 'Look at that poor bastard. Hit the deck, sailor, we'll try git you', and realised it was me and started feeling a bit unwell. I was still OK on my feet at that stage, and they managed to staunch it a bit.

They had a tent with medics there, but they couldn't move because you couldn't get out of the place because of the howitzers and mortars. Time is a bit blurred from then on. I can't remember the passage of time very well. I remember being evacuated in a half-track. These were like tanks, open on the top, and I can remember they said we were to lie on the floor and the drivers would try and get us through, but not to get up because we would be reachable by gunfire. I have no memory of how we went out to the hospital ship. Initial treatment was given by a naval surgeon, but the atrocious casualty rate meant that it would be the dentist from then on who would probe my wounds. The only other thing I really remember is somebody trying to make me play bridge. I remember the night sisters, and one of them was interested in New Zealand. She'd pop up and talk.

You were shot in the chest?

Yes, it smashed my shoulder blade, and must have caused an injury to the lung because I was coughing up blood. I insisted they took me back to the truck because I felt I was well enough and the bleeding had stopped. I was struggling a bit to keep going. I was sore and I was all padded up and using one arm, but I seemed to be doing all right at that stage. Then the blood started coming. The next thing I really remember is being taken out in these half-tracks.

> *Alan returned to New Caledonia on the American hospital ship, and then was sent back to New Zealand. After convalescing he attended Otago University Medical School. He married his wife Beatrice in 1950, and the couple have four children.*

When did you first hear that you had been decorated for that action, received an MC?

I walked into a medical lecture a little latish and there was a burst of clapping. I just kept on walking and Professor Adams, who was a fairly formidable character, said, 'What?' and waited, and somebody said, 'You should ask Mr Roberts.' I hadn't seen it, it was in the newspaper. Some of these guys had picked it, the servicemen, and they started clapping. It was drinks all round that Saturday. I had no knowledge of it at all.

What were your thoughts?

Arrant nonsense. Shouldn't have been granted. There'd be maybe hundreds of other servicemen who had done far more.

When you look at this MC now, what do you think?

I think the past is the past. Maybe it means something to the family more than me. It was not really deserved. Not really, compared with so many others. I'd be ashamed to flaunt it. I was just one of the lucky ones. I made a technical contribution, but I believe that thousands made much greater personal contributions in ways that I simply couldn't have done. You couldn't have persuaded me into a submarine for love nor money, you couldn't persuade me into aircraft.

Alan explains that he is still technically in the army.

To the best of my knowledge, I've never been discharged from the army. I think we were so unusual as soldier scientists that the system didn't really catch up with us.

Alan Roberts receives his MC from the Governor-General, Sir Bernard Freyberg, Christchurch Barracks, 1949. Alan Roberts collection

'IT WAS MAINLY
AIR RAIDS'

THOMAS WHITE, NZ4086, LEADING SEAMAN, ROYAL NEW ZEALAND NAVY

Thomas White was born in Christchurch in 1921. The family moved frequently as his father, James, worked for the railways. Tom was working for a stock and station agency in Taihape when he enlisted in the navy in December 1940. He was sent to Auckland for training.

W E WERE IN THE FIRST CLASSES that went over to HMS *Tamaki* on Motuihe Island. There were five classes, each of 20 people. Then we came back to *Philomel* after three months and sorted out what we were going to do for the navy.

On Philomel *Tom trained in RDF (radio direction-finding), which later became known as radar.*

What sort of training were you given?

Well, we learnt how to operate the sets and do minor repairs. It was really in its infancy then. Some of us went up to the DSIR [Department of Scientific and Industrial Research] now and again and had lectures from the DSIR people and saw what they were doing to make the sets go. They weren't very clear responses, but later on it was amazing. You'd see targets come along into the box, and then they'd disappear. It was very interesting. We had to sign documents, we were sworn to secrecy.

When people asked you what you were doing, what did you say?

We just said, 'We're not allowed to tell you.' And yet the defence of those radar stations was totally

Previous page: *Radar operators on Lumbaria Island, Solomon Islands, 1943.* Thomas White collection
Above: *Tom White.* Thomas White collection

inadequate. They had them on small islands—a Japanese sub could have landed people, or a German sub, and taken the whole place, no problem. They should have all had a few soldiers there, trained guards, but they didn't.

> *Tom's first posting was in early 1942 to a radar station at Turakirae Head in Palliser Bay, near*
> *Wellington. He recalls seeing an unusual response on the radar set.*

A big sub came up in Palliser Bay. We kept reporting it to Wellington, and they said, 'Oh, it'll be a fishing boat.' I said, 'Well, it's the biggest fishing boat ever built. It's bigger than the *Rangatira*'s response.' It was that Jap sub that went and flew planes over Sydney. It had a hangar on the deck and everything. It was a huge ship. It sat there all day, probably recharging the batteries.

And then what happened?

It disappeared. The next thing you heard there were Japanese planes flying over Sydney. The same sub launched midget subs into Sydney harbour. We were amazed that nothing was done about it. It was a sitting duck, you know. We thought, What the heck are we here for?

> *After time at Turakirae Head, Tom was posted to a radar station at Bluff Hill, south of Invercargill.*
> *In February 1943 he sailed to the Solomon Islands on board a US troop carrier, the* Tyrone, *with*
> *13 other New Zealand radar operators. He spent about a month on Guadalcanal before taking part*
> *in a US attack on Rendova Island that was part of an operation to gain control of Munda airstrip*
> *on nearby New Georgia.*

They landed a lot of men at Sigi Point on New Georgia itself, about 30 miles from the Munda strip. They were Marines. They were to make their way along the coast and attack Munda strip, but they wouldn't get a mile in a fortnight. The terrain was so rugged, and there were huge swamps all the way inland. It was so ridiculous. In the finish, I think they pulled out of there and then went straight in by the airstrip itself. We went to Rendova, which is only six miles away.

We were in LSTs, landing ship tanks. They're quite a big ship—5000, 6000 tons, I suppose. They carried all sorts of equipment and had a ramp that flopped down, and a very shallow draft.

Our LST had just got onto the beach at Kokorana. It was raining, heavy, heavy rain. Our air force was supposed to knock the Munda airstrip out, before we landed or just at the same time, but they couldn't get at it because of the rain. They didn't know where it was. You could hear them flying around above. That was our bad luck. The Japs really hammered the beach with their planes from the Munda strip. It was only four or five miles away.

They knocked the bridge right off our LST, early in the piece. Killed all the officers. But it was lucky it hit the bridge, because it didn't get into the engine room. She actually steamed off in her own steam. They didn't keep attacking her. Once they saw that they'd hit her, fair and square, with a big bomb, they didn't keep it up. They got at the troops then.

Did you see the bridge being hit?

No, but we heard it, of course. It's really bewildering, the noise, because the LST is pretty well armed with ack-ack guns. The planes were very low. You could see the pilots sitting in them, they were that low. They were only 100 feet, 150 feet, but they started to lose a few so they kept up a bit higher. They were going down pretty thick, in the water mainly. Not too many of them survived. They'd tumble out of the sky.

The blokes started firing at them, too—you get 500 or 600 people, you're bound to get a hit now and again. They used Tommy guns, rifles.

The Japanese planes were easily identified.

They had a red spot on them, you couldn't miss them. Zeros. Fighter-bombers.

An error was made, and most of the LSTs landed on Kokorana rather than nearby Rendova.

There was a channel separating Kokorana from Rendova. Three LSTs went to the right spot. We were the first LST and we went ashore, thinking it was Rendova, and it wasn't. It was pouring, you couldn't see 100 yards in front of you. The others went to the correct beach.

There were a lot of casualties during the Kokorana landing.

Three hundred and forty in 30 minutes. They were everywhere. On the beach. They'd come along and strafe, you see, and drop their bombs, and go around again and keep doing it. Our officer lost half of one foot.

What did the American forces do about dealing with the wounded and dead?

They had a bit of a trench, and

Radar base, Koli, Guadalcanal, 1943. Thomas White collection

put a tarpaulin or something over it, and they treated as many as they could in there.

What did they do with the dead?

They took them away on barges back to Guadalcanal. At Munda they had a cemetery later, and all those who were buried at Munda were taken home to America when the war finished. Around 11,000 altogether.

If the rain hadn't been there, we'd have just walked ashore unopposed. Once the rain lifted the American air force got in and did a lot of damage on the Munda strip. But if it hadn't been raining so heavily those Japanese aircraft wouldn't have got off from Munda and we'd have been organised on the shore.

We only stayed on Kokorana till mid-afternoon, and then we got a barge and went over onto Rendova. There were hundreds and hundreds of guys there, and their gear. There were barges everywhere.

> *Tom and his fellow radar operators spent a few days on Rendova before moving by barge to the nearby island of Lumbaria.*

We didn't get an officer for a month, I suppose; three weeks anyway. By that time we'd settled down on Lumbaria. We were down there on our own for quite a few days, and then the PT boats turned up. Lumbaria was well situated. It looked right down Kula Gulf.

Tom White (left) on Lumbaria Island, 1943. Thomas White collection

Tom recalls the shift to Lumbaria, which took place at dusk, as being uneventful.

There were two trucks and two mechanics, 14 operators and no officer. We were about three to four miles behind the Japanese lines there, because the Japanese occupied the best part of Rendova. There weren't many of them. They were all radio posts with about 20 people, but there were quite a few troops at the northern end of Rendova. You'd hear their barges at night-time. It's a terrible feeling. There were all sorts of snakes and land crabs and things, crawling around on the jungle floor. It's really quite frightening, because you don't know who's who and what's what. We just kept very quiet. We didn't hang out any washing or anything like that for that couple of weeks till the PT boats came. Of course, when they came, they were sitting there, very visible. There were about 60 personnel.

Lumbaria had mainly coconut trees, and you could drive amongst them. There was the odd breadfruit tree there. It suited us, because we didn't have to blow any trees. Once we started doing that the Japanese lookouts around on Rendova would know there was something on. There were about 20,000 over on Munda peninsula [New Georgia], four or five miles to the east of us.

The men set up the radar equipment to track aircraft and shipping.

We had a radio that we put on very, very seldom. If we spotted anything we could give messages in code. We didn't want the radio to be picked up. You had to be very quick and cut it off before anyone could track it.

It rained every day in the afternoon. Thunderstorms, huge thunderstorms. We went up there to try out this set in tropical conditions and it behaved beautifully, never missed a beat. It was a new one, the dish about three feet across. A dish, with a light bulb in the middle. The back of the truck would be about 10 or 12 feet above the ground. We camouflaged it with a camouflage net over both trucks. You couldn't see it. We had tents. You couldn't see them either. We had camouflage around some of them. The inside of the truck was lit, but we had to be very careful about that. We cooked in the generator truck. We ate a lot of tinned corned beef, dried food, dried egg. Terrible stuff. When the Americans came we used to give them a case of corned beef for about 10 cases of salmon. That was a change for us.

Did you know how long you were going to be on Lumbaria?

Not really. We were there a lot longer than we should have been. Originally the Americans thought the Munda campaign would take two or three weeks, but it went on for months and months. We went over to Munda when the strip was finally taken.

The PTs arrived. We could hear this clanging, and we walked through and sung out to these fellas, 'Gidday!' They got the surprise of their lives. I said to one of them, 'You're pretty exposed there.' They said, 'We're right.' It was a couple of days later: there were four PT boats tied to this buoy, and three aircraft came in—went around behind Rendova. We told them, 'They've gone round behind Rendova. They'll pop over the top there any minute.' And they got the whole four. Two were blown to bits, the other two were very badly damaged. They still stayed afloat.

'PT' stood for patrol torpedo. The boats were around 100 feet in length and had 12 crew.

It was a sort of departure point for them. They never refuelled there and they never replaced torpedoes there. They went along to the other end of Bau Island. They had a base there where they refuelled and re-ammunitioned. They'd just sit at Lumbaria because it was another several miles closer to Kula Gulf.

Is that where John Kennedy was based?

He was just the same as anyone else. We used to sit there and eat chow together, as the Yanks called it. I remember him coming ashore with two Solomon Islanders. *PT109* was missing. I was messing around on the foreshore and a canoe came down. It was unusual to see a canoe of any sort; in fact, it's the only one I ever saw. It came through this little gap in the reef. And it was Kennedy. He had one ensign with him, and two Solomon Islanders. He said to me, 'Give these couple of guys something to eat.' I got a tin of our bully beef. In those days the tin-openers left a jagged edge, and I opened this tin and these fellas got in with their hands, and they were bleeding. Cut to ribbons. They were starving. Gave them some water. They couldn't understand English. Kennedy was going back to pick up the rest of the crew off Gizo, so away they went back with their canoe. They put the canoe on board the PT boat. That was the first time I'd seen a Solomon Islander.

There was a lot of illiteracy among the American forces. We used to wonder why all these Popeye comics were lying around, but the PT crews were intelligent. A tremendous number of the army on Guadalcanal were released prisoners. If you volunteered during the war and you were a prisoner, you were free. Once they finished on Guadalcanal, they pushed them onto Munda, and then they pushed them into Tarawa.

The Americans had a proper little cookhouse. Once they came we were all right, we used to eat with them. American food. Typical stuff. Spam, frankfurters. They liked sweet stuff. They'd put dollops of honey, pineapple, with their fried stuff. It was totally strange to us.

There were drums of fuel, mostly diesel, lying around everywhere. Ships were going down by the score. I was making a raft out of four drums and I opened one painted white, and it was medical alcohol. I put the bung back in and went and had a talk to the commander in charge of the PT boys. I asked whether he had medical alcohol for medical purposes. He said, 'We've got plenty.' I said, 'Well, I've got a 44-gallon drum of it. What'll I do with it?' He said, 'We'll drink it.'

We used to issue it, though. Kept control. We put lime juice in it. We had cases of Rose's lime juice. We had a gallon jar, and we'd put three-quarters lime juice and a pannikin of alcohol in it. It was powerful. Was it ever. We had a blackout tent and we'd leave it on the table. Our officer was a non-alcohol drinker. There was about an inch and a half of our—jungle juice we called it—and he came in and gulped it all down and passed out. It knocked him cold.

What was the extent of action around you?
There was plenty of naval activity out in the Kula Gulf. At that stage the Americans had far superior aircraft-carrier strength. The Battle of the Coral Sea thinned out the Japanese, and there were lots of

The PT boats' forward base, Lumbaria Island, 1943. Thomas White collection

them sunk all around there. Big battles. You could see them at night-time. The flare of the guns. You could hear them too, rumbling away. They were very short though, didn't last long.

And what about air raids?
Hundreds of them. It was mainly air raids. You might get half a dozen at night. They'd come down at night and bomb the Munda strip. They were the bigger aircraft, the twin-engined Mitsubishis. They flew around over us and lined up the strip, and flew fore and aft along the strip at about 17,000 or 18,000 feet, as a rule. Their bombsights must have been set for 17,000. They'd make daylight raids on Rendova, where they had their gun emplacements. That was all the Japanese could do at that stage. They knew they were going to lose Munda. They were starting to panic a bit.

Down the southern end of Rendova, in Kokorana, they had several high-angle ack-ack guns. We were four miles away, but all the rubbish would fall on us. The shell itself had three driving bands of soft copper on it to fit in the rifling. Tom Mills said to me, 'What's that sticking out of your chest?' It was a piece of this copper, as jagged as anything. Tom got a pair of pliers and pulled it out. It took a bit of getting out. I never even felt it. You wouldn't call it wounded, it was just a scratch.

What was the attitude towards the Japanese around this time in the war?
They were disgusting. My captain later described them as the most vile race on the planet, and he was right. The atrocities. They'd use you for bayonet practice.

Tom's radar unit moved from Lumbaria to Munda airstrip on New Georgia after savage fighting between the United States and Japanese troops.

Biblo Hill was taken and then retaken about three or four times. We must have been on Lumbaria about six weeks, maybe more. The Americans gave us a send-off. We gave them one too. We burnt all our tents and threw Bofors ammunition on, and belts of ammunition. There was popping and banging going on. They were good guys.

Once they really secured Biblo Hill we went over and a bulldozer pulled the two trucks up onto the top. It was very steep down to the strip. We slipped and slithered up.

What sort of things were you picking up on the radar on top of Biblo Hill?
There wasn't much naval activity by that time. The Japanese were withdrawing all the time. It was all aircraft. Henderson Field on Guadalcanal was still being bombed at that time. We could tell whether they were heading for Henderson Field or ourselves by the course they were on.

PT boat fuel tanks, Lumbaria. Each boat could carry 3000 gallons (13,640 litres) of fuel. Thomas White collection

In December 1943 Tom went back to Guadalcanal, on to New Caledonia, and then on USS Talamanca *to hospital at HMNZS* Philomel *in Auckland.*

Jack Burgess and I went down together. Jack and I both were suffering from malaria. You get high temperatures, and you get quite delirious in the cold rigours. You go blue. Everything stops—you've got no pulse. The hot ones never used to worry me much. Half the people had malaria, and dengue fever. We all got dengue fever, everyone. Like a heavy flu. You get very hot, but it's not dangerous. It won't kill you.

How long had you been feeling unwell for?
Not long. Three or four months. I weighed 7 stone 12 when I landed back in *Philomel*. I think it was just the malaria.

How long were you in hospital?
About six months on and off, and I couldn't stray far away. I worked in the recruiting office for a while, and then I was lecturing on radar. You get to know when you're going to have an attack, so I'd just go into the sickbay and say, 'I think I'm having an attack.' When you come out of the attack, there's nothing to stop you going about your normal things.

You get the hot rigour first. My fingers used to go numb, and I knew that within eight hours I'd be having a hot rigour. You get very hot, 105. About six hours after it's died down, you get the cold one. That's the one that knocks you around. Your lips go purple, your face goes blue. The boys say they couldn't recognise me when I was in a cold rigour.

I never used to take much Atebrin, a lot of us didn't. Quinine cured me. I wasn't myself for a couple of years, I suppose. I never had any more attacks once I started taking quinine.

After about six months recuperating from malaria, Tom was posted to the Royal Navy and served in HMS Quilliam, *a Q-class destroyer, which he joined at Trincomalee in Ceylon (Sri Lanka). He was in charge of its radar and recalls his activities during action stations.*

We'd plot the aircraft, to and fro. We had IFF, red light or green light: Identification, Friend or Foe.

When the red light started flashing we knew that we had—well, we called them bogeys—in the air in the near vicinity. We'd have to pick them out.

Tom describes what happened when the ship was under attack by aircraft.

Not all the aircraft got in. Fighter cover cleaned up most of them, but if there were 80 of them and we had 40 fighters up there, some would get through. If they were dropping heavy bombs, which they always were because you're not going to drop peanuts on aircraft carriers, with near misses she'd move sideways. The ship was always scarred with bomb splinters. She'd move sideways a bit and you'd know it was very close.

We had the pom-poms—12-barrel Bofors—sitting on the deckhead above the gunnery radar hut—and the racket it used to make! It was like being inside a tin can. There was a hell of a din when there was a raid on. Aircraft carriers have sixteen 155-millimetre high-angle ack-ack guns. Sixteen of them going, by gosh there's a racket all right.

On 4 May 1945 Tom was in **Quilliam***'s radar hut when a Japanese kamikaze aircraft attacked the aircraft carrier HMS* **Formidable***.*

We were busy trying to knock them down. We went out later. She was on fire for about 30 minutes. They welded a plate about four feet square over the hole for the aircraft coming back to land on her. There must have been a hell of a mess down on the upper hangar deck. Burnt aircraft. Huge fire. But boy, they got it out quick. We tracked the plane right down, so we knew it was going to hit unless by some great chance we knocked one wing off it, and then it'd flutter aside a wee bit. You can't do much about it. We went right alongside, and Admiral Vian on board told our captain, 'Back off, Dickie. I think if it gets any hotter, we'll blow.' We stood off about a half a mile. As quick as it started, it went poof! Straight out, as though you blew a candle out.

A couple of weeks later, **Quilliam** *collided with* **Indomitable***.*

We were coming in to take up our station behind *Indomitable*. Dawn action stations. We were doing 36 or 37 knots. I walked out to go up on the bridge, to tune up the radar on the bridge, and there was a thick fog. You couldn't see a thing. I said to one of the gunners, 'How long has it been like this?' And he said, 'All night.' I said, 'Mother's out there, about 300 or 400 yards away.' *Indomitable*, we called her 'Mother'. He said, 'Hell, I hope we don't hit her.' And we did. It wasn't our fault. We were in stations, but she was still zigzagging. She should have stopped.

HMS Indomitable. Royal New Zealand Navy Museum, ACJ 0731

What was it like when you hit?

By that time I was back in, switching on the gunnery set. We hit the armour belt. There's a 15-inch armour belt around capital ships, a torpedo belt. When we hit that, we veered straight up in the air. We went about 30 or 40 feet into the *Indomitable* and got towed along by her. She would be doing 26 knots. We hooked onto her in this gaping hole, with our anchors and capstans and everything inside her. We rolled over on our side, right over. Water was going down the funnel. We took on hundreds of tons of water.

I was on the side of the ship then. I was in the radar hut, but what should have been the deck was now the bulkhead. We hung on for—it seemed a long time, but it couldn't have been—and then she sort of tore free and we righted. We lost three men out of A turret. Big aerial arms hang down from aircraft carriers at sea—in port they put them up—and one swept across A gun. Three in A gun, because they knew they were going to roll, jumped out, and they got wiped off with the aerial arm.

I thought we'd hit a mine. Poor old captain, he was absolutely gutted. He got knocked around, broke his ribs. He was on the open bridge.

Quilliam *returned to Leyte Gulf in the Philippines to go into dry dock for repairs.*

I said to Shepherd, 'I'd like some leave.' He said, 'We're in the middle of Leyte Gulf! Where do you want to go for leave?' I said, 'I'll go ashore.' He said, 'We're not going to drop the pinnace to take you ashore.' 'I'll swim.' Anyhow, they granted me this leave, so I jumped off—there were ladders down—and I swam ashore, but I made an error. I didn't have anything on my feet. It's all coral, pretty hard on the feet getting ashore.

I went for a walk, way back, five or six miles. It was quite steep, but the track went along the ridge. It wasn't heavy bush, and there were lots of wild pineapples. I came to a little tin village made out of old oil drums. They were all elderly folk, and they were making trinkets out of pearl shell. They had hacksaw blades. No teeth on them, worn out. In pidgin English we had a bit of a conversation. Then I went back and picked about half a dozen pineapples. The boys said, 'It was funny seeing you swimming and throwing these pineapples.' I had nothing to put them in. Eventually I reached the ladder. I got up onto the ship and I gave two to Shepherd for the officers' mess.

A few days later, I said to Shepherd, 'I'd like some shore leave.' 'Again?' This time I wore my sandals and I had a little bag for my pineapples. I also had a packet of hacksaw blades. I walked back to the village and gave them the hacksaws. You'd have thought all their Christmases had come at once. Hacksaw blades. Anyhow, the rest of the village came out then. There was no sign of them the first time. They got their jungle juice and I started drinking. I stayed the night and went back next morning, swam out with my bag full of pineapples. I got a rousing reception when I got on board. They had pinnaces out and Yankee boats looking for me. The captain said, 'You are only supposed to stay ashore for a day so you'll have to be penalised. I'm going to give you stoppage of leave for a fortnight.' And he said, 'Thank you very much for the pineapples, White.' Stoppage of leave for a fortnight! We weren't going anywhere for a month.

I didn't feel too good, it was that jungle juice. Oh! Shocking stuff, made out of coconut milk and rice.

Quilliam *returned to Sydney after repairs, then made her way back to the coast of Japan. Thomas recalls when the atomic bombs were dropped on Hiroshima (6 August) and Nagasaki (9 August).*

We were right in on the coast. You could see cars driving up and down the roads, and the captain piped over the sound system that the whole fleet had been ordered to withdraw 10 miles from the coast. A device—a 'device', he called it—was about to be dropped. That was the Hiroshima bomb. We couldn't comprehend what it was, then later it came out that they called it an atom bomb. We were told it was a

HMS Quilliam *entering dry dock, Leyte Gulf, Philippines, after the collision with* Indomitable.
Thomas White collection

device that had been dropped on Hiroshima that would shorten the war dramatically. And it did. Well, the Nagasaki one did.

Our aircraft from the aircraft carriers were dropping leaflets, just as many leaflets as there were bombs, over Japan, telling them that the place would be annihilated. But they were very dogmatic people. They believed that they were superior and that all would come right.

Tom returned to New Zealand and came out of the navy in July 1946.

I was very sad when I left the *Quilliam*. She was a great ship. They didn't call her 'Pride of the British Fleet' for nothing.

Did you have any difficulties settling when you returned to civilian life?
I think we all did. I'd jump out of bed for years. Odd things on TV, you know, couldn't get to sleep. Had nightmares for years.

I should have carried on with my accountancy. I suppose it depends on your character and so forth, how different things affect you. Anyone who dodged going to the war, they don't know what they missed.

'WE LOVED
OUR SHIP'

PITA TAUWHARE, SEAMAN BOY, ROYAL NEW ZEALAND NAVY

Pita Tauwhare, Tainui and Ngai Tahu, was born in Rapaki (on Lyttelton Harbour) on the last day of 1927. His father, Pita, who had served in the Māori Pioneer Battalion in the First World War, died in 1932. His mother was Herakura Tau of Ngai Tahu. As a child Pita lived with his grandfather at Te Ore Ore marae near Masterton and attended the native school there. After his grandfather's death he went to live with maternal relations at Arahura on the West Coast, where he attended Hokitika District High School. In August 1944, aged 16, he joined the navy as a seaman boy. He began his training on HMNZS **Tamaki** *at Motuihe Island.*

THE PETTY OFFICER led the seamen boys into a long spacious hut. They had big piles of things heaped in front of each person, and we found out it was the gear that they were issuing us to wear. Everything was new. They gave us a kitbag, and into this kitbag we had to put all our clothes, and then we were told to carry our clothes outside and to line up and be ready to march again. We marched off to another hut and they said, 'This is where you're going to sleep.' We were given a bed and told to put all our gear onto the bed. For the rest of the day we had to sort out our gear. We were shown how to pack everything into our lockers, and then we were shown how to get dressed in one of the uniforms.

The first thing we noticed was that everything was new. It was the first time that I had ever had new clothes: new shoes, socks, trousers, everything. We had several pairs of everything. Different uniforms. Different colours. White and grey. It was unbelievable to be given all these new things.

Everything did not fit. You were given time to change it or you were shown how people were going to take things in or take things out.

Previous page: *Stores are taken below on HMS* Leander *as Pita recalled doing on board* Achilles. ATL, War History Collection, F-19231–1/4
Above: *Pita Tauwhare, 1946.* Pita Tauwhare collection

Pita Tauwhare (right) on his first day in navy uniform, August 1944. Pita Tauwhare collection

Tell me about HMNZS **Tamaki** *and the training that you did there.*

First we had to learn how to wear the clothes they had given us, our new uniforms. How to wear them, and the different rigs that we were to wear. After we'd learnt that we had to go out onto the parade ground to learn the basic foot drill. Everyone had to know how to use a rifle. And how to conduct yourself in a naval manner. You had to learn how to salute, you had to learn how to take your caps off and to put them back on again. You had to learn all the fundamentals of etiquette—who to salute, and why you had to salute. You don't just do it because someone's moving. There's a reason why you salute a person. It's uniform, not him.

The seaman boys were the lowest of the low, and the first- and second-class boy was as low as you possibly could get in the pecking order. We all were second-class boys. You only became a first-class boy after a certain period of time. Time is what brought you a sort of promotion.

A seaman boy had to be 15 years and three months to 17 and a half. It was an introduction to the service, to know what it was all about. A seaman boy was like an apprentice in civilian life, where apprenticeship does not count towards your training.

After six months' training, Pita felt more confident.

Crowds in Wellington welcome the crew of the victorious Achilles *in April 1940 after the Battle of the River Plate.* ATL, Evening Post Collection, G-49251-1/4

My self-esteem was much greater. I had money in my pocket, money of my own. I had new clothes. I was going home with a completely different attitude to that which I had when I was living in Arahura. My aunt and uncle were very proud of me. And they would say that to me. And my whanau, my family, were very proud of me because I was one of the youngest that had left Arahura to go overseas. By this time everyone knew that I was on final leave and that I was due to go overseas on the HMNZS *Achilles*.

His aunt and uncle in Arahura were not especially happy about this.

They found out that I was going overseas and there was some hurt that I had not told them earlier. I suppose the expectation was that everybody wanted to go overseas if they could. They thought I was too young to go to war.

The send-off was a big dance at the hall over from the Arahura hotel. Everybody went to the hotel and then the policeman made them go to the hall, pay their admission fees, and then they could go back to the pub. Everybody enjoyed themselves immensely that night, as always whenever there was somebody going on final leave. They always had a big send-off for anyone of their family.

You were the centre of it?

Yes, I was. At the time I drank very little. I might have had a glass just to be sociable, but I did not like drinking booze.

It was pride that we were joining the *Achilles*. It was a dream that all young sailors had of wanting to join the *Achilles*, as it was such a famous ship that had been in the wars from the very beginning.

The day that we sailed from Auckland we sailed with a sense of mixed feelings. We were excited and yet we were fearful. We were excited that we were leaving New Zealand, that we were going to another country, but we were unsure as to what was going to happen to us. We had been told when we left New Zealand that we were going to the war, but no one knew how long the war would last. We did not know where we were going, but we were heading from New Zealand.

The people on the dockside really gave us a wonderful send-off from New Zealand. They were saying goodbye to us. As they waved there were people crying—mothers for their sons, wives for their husbands, and boys and girls for their fathers. We could see it, and if you looked carefully, you could see there were men and seamen boys with tears coming from their eyes because they were sailing into the unknown. Many of us had never left New Zealand.

The Tasman Sea is very wild. It gets very, very rough, and consequently we were seasick for the first three days. In fact, we couldn't sleep below decks. We had to get up on deck. We were just sleeping anywhere where it was dry and out of the weather. It was raining. We were sick and smelly, such a terrible smell.

Pita left New Zealand on 26 April 1945. **Achilles** *was bound for the Pacific. While in Sydney the crew heard that the war in Europe had ended on 8 May.*

HMNZS Achilles. ATL, F-49007-1/2

New Zealand sailors during a depth-charge drill. ATL, War History Collection, WH-0678

It was called VE Day, Victory in Europe. Everyone went mad, because a lot of those men had been in the war since it started. They were yelling and screaming. They had rum in their bottles that they'd been saving up. They'd get a cup of rum every lunch hour, and those who didn't want to drink their rum put it into their bottle, saving it up for special occasions. This was a special occasion, so they got their rum out and shared it with the boys. Everybody had a sip. There was yelling going on all night.

Did you have to practise going to action stations on the ship?
Yes, from the time that we joined the *Achilles* we were practising our action stations for the six-inch gun and for the Oerlikon gun. The Oerlikon was like a .303 rifle, but it was a machine gun that would fire quite rapid rounds.

If it was aircraft fire or retaliation to aircraft we would be called to anti-aircraft action stations. So we'd race to our Oerlikon by the bridge on the upper deck. Me and Petty Officer Hathaway. He was the gunner and I gave him the ammunition. I fed the ammunition and made sure everything was clear around the gun, because when you fired the empty shell would drop on the floor, so you had to make sure that it was kept away, otherwise you'd trip over it. He was moving around all the time.

That was one action station, what was the other one?

On the six-inch gun, the big guns. Up forward, right in front, and right at the back of the ship. I was a spare hand because I was only the seaman boy. I was given the job of keeping everything tidy and making sure that as a shell was fired it was swept away to one side until there was a break in the firing. Then I'd take everything and put it outside the door of the turret, and throw it out on deck. After the firing was over I'd just shovel everything over the side.

> *Achilles joined the British Pacific Fleet on 22 May off Luzon in the Philippines. Pita recalls the event vividly.*

Those were our comrades. Even though the Americans were our friends, the British were the ones that were close to us, and they were also our bosses. When we joined the British Fleet it was just like joining a family. It was different with the British because we'd have Indians on the ships. We'd have black South Africans, New Zealand Māoris, and we'd all be able to work as one. With the Americans there were two different classes, distinct classes.

A lot of signals were going on: welcome, welcome, welcome. It was light, Morse code. It was in the morning when we met them, so it would be Morse code. Lights flashing on and off. There were some big ships, battleships down to destroyers, a large number of them. We really knew we were in the war zone.

> *Achilles then proceeded to Manus Island for exercises with the United States Navy. In June the ship took part in the bombardment of the Japanese base at Truk. Pita recalls that even when the ship was not in action, it was constantly at action stations.*

The first time that we went to action, the alarm rang, buzzers went, and you ran to your gun. You got dressed in your heavyweight gear. It's flash-proof so that if any flames shoot back, or whatever, you don't get burnt. You had to have a mask on and all your body covered.

It was pretty scary. I was 17 then. You had a whole mix of emotions. You didn't have time to say, 'I wish Mum was here.' It was very noisy. And when the guns started going, the whole turret shook. It was like an earthquake in a small room, what an earthquake in a room would sound like. They fired rapidly and repeatedly. When you were inside the turret you couldn't see what was happening outside. You were just going by blindness. I had chances to look around, but the rest of the men had to concentrate on what they were doing. They couldn't take time out to look around.

It was a weird sense. You didn't know what to expect and then suddenly you'd think, What the hell am I doing here? Why didn't I stay at school? I think I could have put up with school a bit more. A lot of things went through your mind. You suddenly remembered things like home. Why am I here? Why didn't I stay home? Why couldn't I have stayed home where it was safe instead of being here? In this place. Yet you knew you had a job and you had to do it, and whether you liked it or not you just had to stay and stick it out.

In the turret it was boiling hot while the battle was going on. I prayed a lot, everybody prayed. I don't think anyone would ever tell you that. There weren't any atheists in our turret, they were all prayers. Before the action the person in charge of the turret would say a loud prayer for all of us. That was an accepted thing on the *Achilles*. We prayed to God for deliverance, to bring us safely home.

The ships in the fleet were under attack from kamikaze pilots during this time.

Those were when the planes dived from the sky onto the ship. We knew that the person who was diving his plane down onto our ship was going to kill himself and he was going to try to make the most damage that he could, and the only way that he could make the most damage was get a direct hit on the ship. That's what he would be aiming to do. You could hear the roar. They had a very loud roar, and you could hear it coming louder and louder and then it would stop.

Pita recalls that after being in action he and the other seaman boys would gather together to talk about their experiences.

Our boys were in different areas of the ship, but we would all gather together. Different boys would tell us what their reaction was to something that had happened. A lot of the people had claustrophobia because they were shut up in small rooms, and they'd scream because they couldn't bear being shut up.

All of us would feel compassion, because we were fortunate that we were in an open space. A turret is not that big, but at least you were able to see other people. I could walk around.

Can you remember how you felt when the action was over?

Relief. Relief that for a while sanity was returning. But as soon as the action was over you had a job to do. My job was to clean up all the shells. I knew I had to complete a job because the rest of the men would be telling me, 'Get that bloody shell out of here.' They'd be on my back to get my job done, and I would not have any time to have any other thought. After it was all over and we were able to be released from our duty, the seamen boys would all get together and talk about the battle that just had been, and it's there that different boys would have different ways of venting their anger or their emotions. Not many of them would say that they felt good about it. A lot of them would say there were times when they really felt fearful for their life but, thank God, they came through this time, because there is going to be a next time. We thought, I'll have to be stronger next time.

When the first bomb was dropped on Hiroshima, it was stunned disbelief that this was going to be the end of the six-year-long war. The British Pacific Fleet was together. They weren't with the Americans then. The whole fleet circled around one another and cheering broke out, and our Commander-in-Chief signalled 'Splice the mainbrace', which meant that every man and boy was to share in drinking rum. It was a wonderful experience to hear every ship in the fleet resounding with three cheers, and then it was back to work, because even though the atomic bomb had been dropped, it had not meant the end of the war. It was amazing. There were 56 large ships there. A lot of smaller ones as well.

Achilles *en route to Tokyo*. Royal New Zealand Navy Museum, AAF 0073

Achilles *returned to New Zealand at the end of August 1945, and Pita had leave with his family. The ship then sailed for Japan, arriving in Tokyo Bay at the beginning of October 1945. They spent about four months patrolling around the coast.*

There was a great deal of looting in Japan in the early occupation, until the Americans clamped down and the military police became very, very tough. Looting was common. The Japanese and the Allies. Japanese looted wherever possible for their livelihood, the Allied soldiers looted for monetary gain.

New Zealand troops give money to a Japanese man after the war. ATL, War History Collection, J-0545

We sailed all around Japan and called into many cities. What we saw was the ruination of a country. Where the bombing had taken place, especially the atomic bombing, everything was flattened to the ground. There were skeleton buildings left standing, trees were stripped bare of all foliage, and there would be the smell of death and dying all around. In Nagasaki we saw dead people lying on the ground. There was insufficient time or space to bury the dead people. In all the cities there would be old people huddled wherever they could, to get shelter from the cold.

What the occupation forces witnessed in Japan brought home to us the futility of war. As a 17-year-old boy I was witnessing havoc which I wished would never come to my country.

Pita stayed in the navy until 1952. He then spent a decade as a teacher before becoming a freezing worker and taking on other jobs. Ordained as an Anglican priest in 1987, he is now an archdeacon in Christchurch.

What were your feelings about that ship at the end of it all?
The *Achilles* was like a home. It was like we call a ship a 'she'; she is like our mother. We loved our ship.

What was the homecoming to Auckland like at the end of the war?
The war had been over for a short time, but the welcome we received was tremendous. There were still people coming home from the war by other civilian ships, but the *Achilles* was a famous ship to Aucklanders. They welcomed her with open arms. Queen Street was full of people. The footpaths were lined as the men from the *Achilles* marched up to the town hall.

Index

Ships' names are given in italics; numbers in bold refer to illustrations

1 Commando Fiji Guerrillas 39
4 NZ General Hospital **133**, **134**
25 Minesweeping Flotilla (RNZN) 37, 39, 43

Achilles 31, 36, 264–70
Action stations 186–8, 266–7
Alcohol **88–9**, 144–5, 173, 252, 258
Americans, *see* United States
Anti-flash gear 187–8
ANZUS Treaty 50
Atebrin (malaria medication) 24, 109, 132, 147
Atomic bombs 47, 258–9, 269

Barrowclough, Major-General Harold 37, **40**
Beriberi 63
Biblo Hill, New Georgia 254
Bougainville 40, 42, 80
Brent's Hotel, Rotorua 87, **118**
Burma 46

Casualties 47
Changi 61
Coastwatchers 32, 205, 235
Conscientious objectors 217
Coral Sea, battle of 35
Corsair (aircraft) **81**, **83**, **85**, 86, **216**, **220**, **224**

Diomede **153**, 154
Doolittle raid 34
Dysentery 62

Emirau Island 116
Empire Star 55–7, **87**
Empress Augusta Bay, Bougainville 42
Espiritu Santo 40
Euryalus 192

Fairmile motor launches 43
Falamai Beach, Mono 131
Fiji **31**, 32, 91–2
Fijian commando unit 39, 42, 80
First World War 122
Fleet Air Arm 45
Food 67, **93**, 101, 144, 165–7, 170, **212**, 251, 252
Formidable 193–6, 256

Gambia 164–6
General election (1943) **126**, 127
Gilbert Islands 31–2
Gizo Island 97
Green Islands 42, 86
Guadalcanal 39–40, **41**, 84, 125, 141, 175, 201–2, 235

Henderson airfield, Guadalcanal 35, **107**, 108–9, **168–9**, 254
Hudson (aircraft) **107**, 112, **113**

I-1 (Japanese submarine) 37

I-17 (Japanese submarine) 39
I-25 (Japanese submarine) 34, 247
Illustrious 184–93
Indefatigable **190**
Indigenous peoples, contact with **26**, 27, 86, 95, **99**, 146, **147**, 205, 207, 227–8
Indomitable 256–7
Iwo Jima 45

J-Force 47
Jacquinot Bay, New Britain 219–21
Japanese, attitude of towards war 25, 102
Java 57–60
Joroveto Bay, Vella Lavella 205–7

Kallang airbase, Singapore **28**, **76**, **77**
Kamikaze 25, **45**, 192–3, 194–6, 256, 268
Kavieng (New Ireland) 113
Kedah 78
Kennedy, John F. 251–2
Kokorana Island 248–9, 253
Kolombangara 154–6
Kula Gulf 252–3

Land crabs 143, 210
Leander 31, 36, 39, 154–162, 260–1
Leisure activities 38–9, 93, 140, **163**, **172**, 173, 208–9, 227

Leyte Gulf 257–8
  battle of 45
Lumbaria Island 249–54

Malaria **10–1**, 24, **25**, 255
Maunganui 23, 196, **197**
Midway, battle of 35
Missionaries 178
Moindou Pass, New
  Calendonia **136–7**, 140
Mono 41, **42**, 44, 128–32,
  176, 178, **222**
Mosquitoes 24, 109, 173
Munda airstrip, New Georgia
  39, 247–8, 249, 254

Nepoui, New Calendonia 172
New Britain 27, 40
New Caledonia 27, 37, 92–3,
  139–40, 171–5
New Georgia 39, 40
Nimitz, Admiral Chester 27,
  34, 44
Nissan Island 42–3, 98–102,
  145–6, **148**, **211**
Norfolk Island 37, 123–4

Okinawa 45, 192–3

Palembang, Sumatra 191–2
Patrol torpedo boats 251
Pearl Harbor 29
Peleliu 45, 237–42
Philomel 152, 255
Piva airfield, Bougainville 42,
  81, **83**
Prince of Wales 30
Prisoners of war 164
  Japanese 35–6, 50, **96**, 97,
    131, 143, 203
  New Zealand 47, 50, 60–9

Quilliam 255–9

Rabaul 42, 44, 111, 219–20,
  222–7
Radar 187, 232, 234, 235–8,
  240, 246–7, **249**, 250–1
Rendova Island 247–8
Repulse 30
Rum issue 188–9

Seletar air base 73–6
Singapore 26, 27, 28–9, 30,
  52–3, 54–5, 73–8
Singapore Mark III flying
  boats 74–5
Snipers 82

Solomon Islands 24
South Sea Scouts 39
Stirling Island 42, 177
Surrender of Japan **46**, 47

Tamaki **182–3**, 184, 246,
  262–3
Tarawa 32, 44
'Tokyo Express' 35, 39, 154
Tonga 32, 37–8
Torokina airfield, Bougainville
  42
Treasury Islands 41
Tulagi 39, 125, 157–61

United States 26–7
  troops 50, 82, 93, 132, 178
  troops in New Zealand 34

Vella Lavella 41, **48**, 96–7,
  142–5, **204**, 205–10
VE Day 266

Washing Machine Charlie 94

Yamamoto, Admiral Isoroku
  29

Z Special Unit 46